MW01031507

The Rookie's Guide to Guns and Shooting, Handgun Edition

What you need to know to buy, shoot and care for a handgun

by Tom McHale

Insanely Practical Guides

Charleston, South Carolina

ISBN 978-0-9890652-3-8

my husband
is
cross dressing
and it
makes
me
so
uncomfortable

Dear Jesus,
I admit

I'd like to dedicate this book to my wife and best friend of many years. I couldn't ask for a more dedicated and supportive partner in these endeavors.

"A wife of noble character who can find? She is worth far more than rubies. Her husband has full confidence in her and lacks nothing of value. She brings him good, not harm, all the days of her life."

Proverbs 31:10-12

But First, A Serious Note

Proper handling and carrying of firearms is serious business. While we at MyGunCulture.com aim (Ha! Pun intended!) to make the shooting world more accessible and understandable with a little humor now and then, we firmly believe that nothing takes the place of face-to-face, real-time training. So use this guide as an educational tool to help you understand some of the basics, but never substitute the contents of a quality publication like this one for the expert advice of a skilled and experienced firearms and personal defense trainer.

Now back to business.

Although this is the Handgun Edition, we'll talk just a bit about rifles and shotguns for clarification in some of the crossover areas. In the not too distant future, look for more Insanely Practical Guides that are specific to rifles, shotguns and shooting accessories.

"In a world 3/5 covered with water, it is wise to learn swimming. In a world of warfare and crime, it is wise to learn firearms."

~ Mike Mollenhour, Frequent shooter, an everyday lawyer, an ex-soldier, and a soon-to-be-world famous author. He exercises the First Amendment about the Second Amendment, liberty, and national defense blogging at www.virtualmilitia.com

In true MyGunCulture.com style, this book is written in literary assault format for your enjoyment — half-cocked but right on target. I hope that doesn't offend your sense of decency and decorum — too much.

Dear Jesus, I admit that
I am a sinner, deserving
of hell. please forgive
me of my sins and
take me to heaven
when I die. I now believe
upon you alone, apart from
all self + righteous works

and religion, as my
~~Personal the~~ Personal
Savior, Thank you
amen

admit you are
a guilty
sinner

Do you believe
that Jesus is
the son of

God who
died upon
the cross

suffering

his precious
blood to
pay for
your
sins?

Table of Contents

CHAPTER 1 - A Brief History of Guns 1

CHAPTER 2 - Rules of Gun Safety 25

    Rule 2 28

    Rule 3 30

    Rule 4 32

CHAPTER 3 - Types of Guns 35

    Handguns 36

    Handgun Action! 50

    Rifles 60

    Shotguns 64

CHAPTER 4 - Things To Consider When Choosing Your First Gun 73

CHAPTER 5 - How to Buy a Gun 77

    Tips For A Successful Gun Store Visit 79

    Buying Guns Online! 85

    Family, Friends and Neighbors 93

CHAPTER 6 - Gun Holsters - Do It Right! 95

    A Gun Holster Tale… 98

CHAPTER 7 - A Few Comments on Gun Handling 101

CHAPTER 8 - A Fistful of Shooting Tips 105

Stand Like You Mean Business.....................107

Learn a Proper Grip 111

Use Natural Point of Aim 117

Become One with Your Front Sight 120

Press, Don't Pull, the Trigger 122

Don't Be All Thumbs...................................124

Rack the Slide Like a Pro............................127

Dry Fire and Practice at Home....................132

Practice with a Purpose 142

What if your gun jams? 146

CHAPTER 9 - Let's Go Shooting!.....................151

A Gun Range Story 152

What to Expect and Bring 154

Shooting Range Etiquette 162

CHAPTER 10 - An Ammunition Primer............167

Rimfire and Centerfire 170

Practice Ammunition 173

Self Defense Ammunition............................176

Reloading 180

CHAPTER 11 - Lights, Lasers and Accessories................183

Night Sights..184

Gun Lights 186

Laser Sights 189

CHAPTER 12 - Care and Feeding of Your Gun 193

Cleaning Your Gun 194

Storing Your Gun...202

CHAPTER 13 - The Second Amendment...........................207

A Second Amendment Fairy Tale 209

Joining the NRA 215

CHAPTER 14 - Cheat Sheets.......................................219

Where to Buy Online 220

Training, Dealers and Shooting Ranges 224

Competitive Shooting 226

Legal Stuff and Resources...227

CHAPTER 15 - Parting Shots.......................................229

CHAPTER 1 - A Brief History of Guns

Guns have been annoying politicians longer than you might think. Before we jump into modern day firearm knowledge, let's take a look at the long and winding road of gun history...

1,100 BC

Legends of the earliest known uses of guns have been passed down through generations of Zoran women. Historians believe that many women folk of Zorah, then near Philistine, gushed and swooned at the sight of Samson's guns. According to the folklore, Samson had two guns, of exceptionally large caliber. Also according to history, he used those guns on more than one occasion - smiting at least one lion and many Philistine warriors. Sadly, the Zoran Congress, led by Senator

Delilah of Timna, Philistia, soon enacted an assault hair ban and Samson was stripped of his guns.

1250 AD

Most historians believe that the key ingredient required to make all those useless guns work was invented around this time. In fact, NRA National Firearms Museum Director Jim Supica claims that Franciscan monk Roger Bacon wrote of the mixture shortly before 1250 A.D. That was an awfully long time ago - just after the birth of Joan Rivers.

Anyway, according to Bacon's ancient texts, the lute and dulcimer trio of Guns and Roses discovered gunpowder while searching for better ways to wow the crowd at outdoor concerts. The forward-thinking band found that a mixture of charcoal, sulphur and salt peter provided plenty of noise and flash for bitchin' stage theatrics. Salt Peter, Saint Peter's long-lost stepbrother, was not at all happy about this recipe and he immediately started work on development of smokeless powders that did not require any of his bodily parts. Progress was slow as smokeless powder was not invented until the late 19th century.

1300

The earliest cannons appeared on the scene. After all, what good was the newly invented gunpowder without something to shoot it from? Early cannons were quite simple - nothing more than a tube open on one end and closed at the other. A small hole near the closed end allowed cannoneers to light a powder charge inside. Crudely constructed from iron, wood and sometimes Mighty Putty, these weapons applied the same basic principles used by guns today.

1350

While loud and impressive, early cannons did little to meet self-defense requirements. Since gun holsters had not yet been invented, concealed carry was not feasible. Hunting with the newly invented firearms was also problematic as many animals were reluctant to stand in front of cannons long enough to be converted to SPAM. In response to complaints of supermarket butchers everywhere, the "hand-gonne" was invented. Simply a downsized cannon mounted on a pole, the hand-gonne struggled for popularity mainly because no one knew how to pronounce the word "gonne."

1400 to 1639

Clearing up name confusion, people stopped making "hand-gonnes" and replaced them with matchlocks and wheellocks. Matchlock guns featured an exposed flash pan filled with fine - and easy to ignite - priming powder, which would light the main charge to fire the gun. A dangling, and lit, fuse was suspended over the flashpan. A mechanical linkage was used to lower the smoldering fuse into the highly combustible flash pan. Occasionally, the matchlocks would fire when the user wanted, but usually before, after or not at all.

1526

The gun company Beretta is founded in the Foccacia region of Italy, in a town called Brescia. Having made guns prior to this date, company founder Ben Cartwright achieves his first commercial success with production of 185 Arquebus Matchlock barrels for the Arsenal of Venice. The British Secret Service, Double-0 branch, is issued the 186th Arquebus. England quietly canceled the Double-0 program when it was discovered that matchlock rifles concealed poorly under dinner jackets.

1640

The first kinda, sorta reliable flintlock was built. Some astute marketers even guaranteed their flintlocks to be 31% reliable, 67% of the time. Offering major advancements in luxury and comfort, such as heated drivers-side seats, the flintlock allowed shooters to carry their guns pretty much anywhere, except schools and government buildings, of course. As the flintlock features a covered flash pan for priming powder, users could even take their guns into rainy conditions. No longer would major World Wars endure rain delays, thereby minimizing network television scheduling challenges.

As a side note, the phrase "keep your powder dry" came into vogue during the flintlock era. As guns of the time relied on ignition of two separate powder charges - one in the flash pan and one in the barrel - keeping powder dry and flammable was a requirement of guns going bang instead of fzzzlpphhtt.

1700's

American pioneers have great success with long, rifled-barrel flintlocks known as Ohio, Pennsylvania and Kentucky rifles. Meddling politicians influenced the design of the California Rifle around this time, but adoption was limited due to the fact that it had no barrel, stock or bullets. As guaranteed 30 minute wild game delivery required great accuracy, early riflemen developed skills with their long rifles.

CONTRARY TO DEVELOPMENT OF THE KENTUCKY RIFLE, MEDDLING POLITICIANS HAD GREAT INFLUENCE OVER DEVELOPMENT OF THE CALIFORNIA RIFLE.

Also during the 1700's, flintlock pistols replaced swords as the personal defense weapon of choice. In fact, flintlock pistol sets were commonly used for dueling. Dueling was a practice where stubborn men shot at each other from close range in order to settle arguments like "tastes great" vs. "less filling." Dueling fell out of vogue in the 19th century when astute practitioners figured out that it really, really hurt to get shot.

1807

Scottish Clergyman and international arms dealer Reverend John Forsyth develops the percussion cap. In addition to providing a fine beat to marching bands worldwide, Forsyth's invention allowed for more reliable ignition of firearm charges. The percussion cap was a small metallic cup, treated with mercuric fulminate - a highly explosive compound that ignites with sharp pressure. With the advent of the percussion caps, guns could be reliably stored in a ready-to-fire condition.

1836

Samuel Colt receives a patent for his revolver design. Horses celebrate as cowboys no longer have to carry the weight of 6 separate single shot flintlock pistols. The Colt design features a revolving cylinder that holds 5 or 6 bullets. Revolvers capable of holding more than one cartridge are immediately banned in New York City. As a result, times are tough for the fledgling Colt company and doors are shut in 1841.

1847

In a corporate resurgence, Samuel Colt teams with Captain Samuel Walker Texas Ranger and introduces the most powerful handgun of the day, after Dirty Harry's .44 Magnum of course. Not wanting to cross Clint Eastwood, the two Samuels abandon plans to name their creation "The Most Powerful Handgun in the World" and call their revolver the Colt Walker. It remained the second most powerful handgun in the world until the introduction of the .357 Magnum 90 years later, at which point Clint Eastwood had shifted focus to making touching romantic films.

1840 – 1870

Up until this time, nearly all guns were "muzzle loaders." This means that powder and projectiles had to be dumped into the muzzle (front end) of the gun, then stomped like wine grapes down into the barrel. Efforts to stomp powder charges and lead bullets down dirty rifle barrels with bare feet greatly slowed down many important battles. While the invention of the percussion cap made a big difference, things were still slow and cumbersome.

Starting in 1840, with the invention of the pin-fire cartridge, guns made the leap from muzzle-loading to breech (back of the barrel) loading. With a self-contained cartridge, shooters could load rifles and revolvers from the back in one smooth motion. No longer did folks have to worry about three separate components - powder, projectile and percussion cap - for each shot.

This reproduction 1858 Remington Bison revolver is an example of a percussion cap revolver. And proof that size matters.

During this era, Colt held the patent for the revolving cylinder concept, which is still the basis for modern revolver designs. However, it was another partnership between Horace Smith and Daniel Wesson that increased popularity of the self-contained cartridge for revolvers. Smith & Wesson obtained a patent for their design and enjoyed a virtual monopoly on cartridge revolvers until 1869.

As a side note, Horace and Daniel dabbled with a lever-action pistol design, but soon scuttled the idea and sold the rights to Oliver Winchester, a shirt manufacturer. Having had his clock cleaned by low-cost clothing firm, Men's Wearhouse, Winchester decided to give firearms manufacture a go.

1866

Overjoyed at scoring two suits for the price of one from Men's Wearhouse, Oliver Winchester releases a series of repeating, lever-action rifles including models 1866, 1873, 1876 and 1886.

1873

Colt begins shipment of its famous Single-Action Army Revolver 1873. Production actually began in 1872, but seeing as Federal Express had not yet been invented, Colt was forced to rely on the Pony Express to fill its distribution channel. This slowed down retail availability considerably. Dubbed *The Peacemaker*, the Colt Single-Action Army Revolver was featured in many great western movies. And many not very great western movies.

Actor Roger Moore is issued a Colt Single-Action Army Revolver for the upcoming James Bond movies, *From Carson City With Love* and *Gold Rush Finger*. Movie production is placed on indefinite hold when Moore fails to come up with a believable cowboy accent. Production assistants also blame the fact that Moore had difficulty walking in chaps without debilitating chafing.

1886

The French Lebel bolt-action rifle is placed into military service. The 8mm Lebel ushered in a new era of military history in that the French actually fielded a weapon. Oh, and the Lebel was the first military rifle to use smokeless powder. Up until this point, battles were often called on account of smoke as opponents could not see each other, or the scoreboard, through the voluminous clouds of black smoke created by gun powder. The advent of smokeless powder allowed battles to proceed in a more orderly fashion. A side benefit of smokeless powder was the ability to propel bullets faster than ever - allowing for longer range and more accurate shooting.

1889 – 1896

Revolvers were here to stay. During this period, both Colt and Smith & Wesson introduced early versions of modern double-action revolvers. The two most important developments were a swing-out cylinder which allowed for easy ejection of spent cartridge cases and load of fresh ones and true double-action operation which allowed shooters to operate the handgun by simply pulling the trigger.

1900

Speaking of swingers, British secret agent James Bond is born in this century. Stay tuned.

1911

In the year 1911, John Moses Browning, may God rest his soul, invented the most powerful handgun ever to be created - the 1911. 1911 pistols have been known to take down both a Japanese Zero fighter and German Storch observation plane in World War II. In fact, some believe that a stray 1911 .45 ACP round inadvertently destroyed the city of Dresden.

Technically, Browning produced a similar design in 1905, but the 1911 was deemed "just about six years better" by industry press.

1915

The Marquis Belt Buckle pistol, also known informally as the Power Pelvis Gun, was conceived by Louis Marquis while interned in a POW camp during World War I. Frustrated by long chow and loo lines, Marquis was consumed by a desire to exert his authority over other POW's without drawing the attention of guards – hence the idea for a concealed weapon not requiring the use of hands or traditional holsters. Named the Koppelschlosspistole, the design was patented before the outbreak of World War II.

In order to gain approval for broad scale deployment, Marquis had to prove that average soldiers could easily be trained to use the weapon effectively. As the pistol had no sights, and relied entirely on groovy pelvic gyration to aim, it was assumed that biological instincts would overcome any training obstacles. And of course, the natural male instinct to aim for the toilet.

Not so, according to WWII historian Basil Exposition. "Training soldiers to charge, while aiming with their pelvises, proved more difficult than anticipated" commented Exposition. "Not only was it nearly impossible to run while aiming one's midsection, it really looked quite effeminate. The enemy was not at all intimidated."

Recent tests have determined that accuracy and effectiveness are increased if Elvis Presley songs are played at loud volume. Unfortunately for the Germans, Presley was not available to train soldiers in proper hip-aiming techniques.

"The Nazis were quite disappointed with early field trials" explained Exposition. "Until they elected to actively recruit accomplished Salsa dancers. However, there were few Salsa dancers in Nazi Germany at the time, and the program was not considered scalable."

Stories of experimental crotch rockets, hula hoop grenade launchers, monocle lasers, and garter garrotes persist; although surviving specimens have yet to be found.

1914 – 1918

World War I marked the advent of the machine gun. Unlike mythical "assault weapons" lamented by politicians and their press corps, actual machine guns often require complete crews to operate and supply them. While most machine guns were heavy and placed in fixed positions, some more portable automatic rifles appeared at the end of the war.

One example was the Browning Automatic Rifle. Designed by John Moses Browning, may he rest in peace, the BAR, or M1918, was intended to be operated by a single soldier. Make no mistake, BAR's were still heavy and cumbersome. In addition to being considered total bro's by their squad mates, BAR men came to war equipped with a cup, as all good privates should. This allowed privates to better protect their privates. Early BAR men were issued an automatic rifleman's belt with a special metal "cup" between the BAR magazine pouches and pistol magazine pouch. This cup was intended to support the BAR's stock as the shooter fired from the hip in a concept called "walking fire."

The idea behind this was to make an automatic weapon portable enough to accompany advancing troops. The Vickers Machine Gun was a tad too bulky and heavy for this use, even by hunks like BAR men, and the Chauchat Machine Rifle, which was portable, was entirely French in terms of reliability and performance. Enough said.

1929 – 1931

The iconic Walther PPK was introduced by Carl Walther GmbH Sportwaffen in 1931. The slightly longer and taller Walther PP had been introduced 2 years prior. Considered by many as the one of the first successful double-action semi-automatic pistols, the Walther PPK quickly gained the approval of spy novel author Ian Fleming. Still produced today, the Walther PPK inspired many modern double-action pistols.

1935

Smith & Wesson introduces the .357 Magnum. Is it coincidence that the Black Sunday dust storms that destroyed the midwest occurred in April of that year? We think not. With the .357 Magnum's muzzle energy exceeding 500 foot-pounds, we think muzzle blast stirred up the dust clouds. Dust storms were immediately banned in all buildings in New York City, with the exception of Department of Motor Vehicles offices.

1939 – 1945

World War II marks widespread use of semi-automatic rifles like the M1 Garand and actual fully-automatic Assault Rifles. The caliber of Assault Rifles was generally less than that of bolt-action or semi-automatic rifles to allow them to be controlled in fully automatic fire.

A World War II classic semi-automatic rifle - the M1 Garand

1949

Firearm entrepreneur Bill Ruger and partner Ben Cartwright score big on the *Wheel of Fortune* progressive dollar slots in Vegas and found Sturm, Ruger and Company. With the belief that Ruger should build each product "to a standard so I would want one even if it was made by our competitors," Ruger risks putting himself out of business, but the investment pays off. In 1990, over the hysterical objections of future New York Mayor Michael Bloomberg, Ruger is listed on the New York Stock Exchange. Bloomberg vows to run for King of New York to rectify the situation.

1955

Smith & Wesson attempts to one-up themselves with introduction of the .44 Magnum. Clint Eastwood's acting career launches into the stratosphere when he utters the immortal line "If you want a guarantee, buy a toaster."

.44 Magnum handguns, like this Ruger Super Blackhawk, pack a serious wallop. While fun to shoot in the movies, real-life shooting requires some dedication!

1958

Fed up with favorite spy hero James Bond's use of a .25 caliber Beretta, Scottish firearms expert, Geoffrey Boothroyd, launches a massive email campaign and Facebook petition against novelist Ian Fleming. After his Twitter followers fall below 10,000 and his Klout score hits negative digits, Fleming relents and equips his fictional character, James Bond, with a Walther PPK in .32 ACP. According to secret agent armorer, Q, the .32 Walther PPK has "a delivery like a brick though a plate glass window." Corning Glass shares immediately increase 23% in after hours trading.

1971

Smith & Wesson CEO Ben Cartwright again stuns the market with introduction of the Smith & Wesson Model 59. Combining double-stack magazine capacity with double-action pistol operation, the Model 59's introduction draws Former Senator Dianne Feinstein out of suspended animation to introduce magazine capacity limit legislation. Unwilling to risk valuation of his Glock founder stock, President Richard Nixon vetoes the bill during a power lunch at Washington's Exclusive Watergate Hotel.

1975

Punk rockers, *The Sex Pistols*, perform their first public concert at St. Martin's College of Art in London. Regardless of having no overseas jurisdiction, Senator Dianne Feinstein immediately files a no-tolerance bill banning the word "sex" from UK colleges.

1982

Curtain rod manufacturer Gaston Glock sees opportunity as the Austrian Army has announced that it requires a new black pistol to complement their ceremonial red berets. Using his background of manufacturing plastic wall hanging utensils, Glock creates the Glock 17, or, as known in other circles, the Glock G.I.L.F. (Glock I'd Like to Fire.) Most historians believe that the Glock 17 was named as it was Glock's 17th patented invention, but in reality, Gaston and crew had to melt down 17 curtain rods to obtain enough black plastic for the prototype pistol.

Referred to as "Tupperware" by detractors, and having little resemblance to their curtain rod roots, polymer Glocks changed the handgun market forever.

2002

Springfield Armory enters into an agreement to produce the XD pistol line. Originally designed by Marko Vuković and his orchestra, the pistol was initially produced for the Croatian Military as early as 1991. Springfield Armory executives intended to meet with Vuković's team, but were delayed by The Croatian War of Independence from 1991 through 1995, thereby stalling the collaborative product launch.

2004

Beretta introduces the PX4 Storm pistol. Featuring space age looks, it offers numerous features to improve comfort, control and accuracy. Replaceable grip panels allow customers to fit the PX4 perfectly to their unique hand size. A novel rotating-barrel recoil design helps keep the PX4 on target by directing recoil straight back instead of "flipping" the muzzle upwards.

The Beretta PX4 Storm combines ergonomic design with proven Beretta reliability. Photo: Beretta USA

2005

Beretta introduces the Tropical Storm Series. The new pistol design represents a quantum leap in weather harnessing technology according to Ben Cartwright, CEO, Beretta USA. "For centuries, we've been developing firearms with energy potential measured in foot-pounds" said Cartwright. "One day while walking my dog Giuseppe in a rainstorm, it occurred to me that we ought to think about harnessing the power of mother nature. When she's upset, things get crazy."

The Beretta Tropical Storm pistol harnesses the power of Mother Nature. When she's upset, things get crazy.

While the previous lineup of PX4 pistols used a creative rotating barrel lockup technology to create a strengthened action with reduced recoil, the new Tropical Storm leverages planetary rotational forces for increased power. Tapping into the power of both hot and cold fronts and lunar gravitation, the first model of the new pistol, the Hugo, is rumored to obtain maximum sustained velocity of at least 63 knots.

"The Gulfstream is a pretty big deal." said Don Draper, Beretta's Vice President of Marketing. "That, combined with the earth's rotation means we don't have to rifle the barrels – and that results in lower costs that we can pass on to our customers."

Draper expects the line to evolve quickly. "As soon as we can break the maximum sustained velocity barrier of 74 knots, we would like to upgrade the line. Maybe we'll name it the Hurricane Storm Series."

2005

Noting that other armies also use red ceremonial berets, Smith & Wesson CEO Ben Cartwright introduces the Smith & Wesson M&P line of polymer pistols. Designed to compete with the Glock, Smith & Wesson's product line offers user-customizable grips, more comfortable handgrip and a deeper shade of black to complement military red color palettes.

2008

Ruger announces its offering to the ultra-compact handgun market - the Ruger LCP. Chambered in .380 ACP caliber, the LCP weighs just 9.4 ounces and fits easily into a pocket. A flood of small and light handguns from various manufacturers follows.

The Ruger LCP offers .380 ACP chambering in a pocket-sized frame. Image: Sturm, Ruger & Company, Inc.

2009

Ruger introduces the Ruger LOP, or Light Origami Pistol. Following the wildly successful introductions of the Ruger LCP, LCR, and LCR .357, the move was the next logical evolution of the Ruger lineup of lightweight and compact pistols according to Ben Cartwright, Ruger's Chief Executive Officer. "From the introduction of the ultra-small and lightweight LCP, our customers have been clear that smaller and lighter is the way to go. And nothing is lighter than origami."

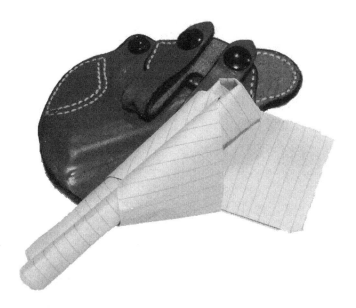

The Ruger LOP (Light Origami Pistol) was literally paper thin.

According to Ruger engineers, the LOP is fabricated from advanced polyfiber composites originally developed for the greeting card industry. While company sources won't comment, it's believed that Ruger has entered a technology licensing pact with greeting card industry giant Hallmark Cards.

While caliber and ammunition details remain unclear, size and weight specifications are impressive. The pistol weighs in at an impressive .003 ounces. Given it's 3mm thickness, the LOP is expected to usher in a new era of concealed carry flexibility.

"There are always design tradeoffs we have to make." continued Cartwright. "In order to meet our size and weight design goals we did have to make some sacrifices in durability. For example, we're recommending that customers in hot and humid climates like Florida refrain from carrying in summer months as excessive humidity and perspiration could weaken the structural integrity of the pistol."

Asked what's next for the newly invigorated company, Cartwright replied "As a publicly traded company we can't comment on specifics, but you might see expansion of the origami design concepts to include things like integrated bayonets and candle illumination units. We're pretty excited about the possibilities of paper as a fabrication material."

2009

Smith & Wesson (SWHC), long time maker of firearms and accessories, experiences a meteoric rise of its share price, resulting in a total market capitalization greater than that of the Federated States of Micronesia. "We could not be more pleased with the recent share price growth" said Smith & Wesson CEO Ben Cartwright. "We're up 87% just since the 2008 election. We're not growing quite as fast as the list of Paris Hilton's ex-boyfriends, but we're getting darn tootin' close."

In related news, Ruger Firearms (RGR) has posted gains of 66% during the same period. Matt Dillon, Executive Vice President of Business Development and Law and Order, notes "That endorsement deal we did with Barak Obama last summer really paid off. We got a fistful of dollars out of that one for dang sure."

Neither CEO would comment on rumors of a hostile takeover of the Island States.

2009

Gun companies find a surprising new market when members of a shooting range encounter an unexpected sight when what appeared to be a TelePrompter was seen shooting handguns and various semi-automatic rifles.

Nearby shooters became suspicious when they overheard the TelePrompter saying "Do you feel lucky? Well, do ya, punk?" Upon hearing this and other obvious movie lines from the Dirty Harry series, nearby shooters decided to investigate.

The shooting community was shaken up when the Presidential Teleprompter was spotted at a local shooting range.

Local resident Bubba "Big Daddy" Dubbelwahd observed the incident. "I was there with my other brother Bubba and his son Bubba, and dang it if I didn't see some TV telespeaker thing down at the end of the shootin' line. Heck I didn't even know they were allowed to own guns."

When questioned, the TelePrompter claimed that it worked for NRA Executive Vice President Wayne LaPierre and was simply there to practice some house clearing drills. Nearby shooters were immediately suspicious of this explanation noting that Mr. LaPierre doesn't require a TelePrompter to formulate coherent thoughts during public appearances. When pressed, the TelePrompter confessed to working for President Barack Obama. "Look, I could get in real trouble for this. My boss isn't real keen on this whole guns and shooting thing, you know, but I just have to get out here once in a while and burn some mad ammo. Plus, I love the smell of gunpowder in the morning. Can we just keep this between us? I'll try and delay that assault weapons legislation if you can manage to keep this quiet."

Local authorities decided that no laws had been broken as TelePrompters are not specifically prohibited from owning firearms.

2010

Chiappa Firearms introduces a new completely upside-down RHINO .357 Magnum revolver. Stunning industry observers, the new revolver announced its intention to caucus with autoloading pistols rather than traditional revolvers.

But seriously, the Chiappa RHINO offers a revolutionary revolver design that helps shooters control recoil as the barrel is lined up with the bottom of the cylinder. This lowers the axis of recoil force.

"We feel shocked" said an obviously stunned Smith & Wesson Classic Model 42. "When you've been around as long as I have you get to expect that the incoming class of freshmen revolvers will stick with tradition and caucus with us."

Most assumed that the inclusion of a rotating cylinder would ensure the RHINO would remain loyal to revolver policy issues. Few expected it to become a Revolver In Name Only, or RINO. "We're just tickled pink about the RHINO's decision" gushed a Smith & Wesson M&P. "Of course, if push comes to shove and a true autoloader wants the job, that RHINO's outta here."

An unexpected benefit of the RHINO .357's decision is a lucrative new prospective base. Political RINO's including Florida Governor Charlie Crist, Maine Senator Olympia Snow, South Carolina Senator

Lindsey Graham, and former Pennsylvania Senator Arlen Specter have all expressed early interest in the **RHINO** .357 revolver. "I was really excited about a revolver that shared my flip-floppy values" commented Specter. "That is until someone told me it was a **RHINO** and not a **RINO**. Bummer."

2010

Smith & Wesson Holding Corporation (SWHC, Nasdaq) announced an extension to it's Bodyguard line of personal protection pistols, the Jersey Shore Edition.

The Smith & Wesson BODYGUARD handgun line features lightweight polymer frames. The polymer construction also reduces felt recoil. Image: Smith & Wesson

Aimed squarely at the post binge-drinking, out of control situation market segment, the Bodyguard Jersey Shore line offers several innovative features designed to offer ego and hairstyle protection, while minimizing regrets the day after.

According to Smith & Wesson CEO Ben Cartwright, the Bodyguard Jersey Shore is designed to protect reputation, ego, and lucrative television contracts without permanent physical harm. "Say you're at the club, at like 3:30am, and some juicehead gorilla wants to smoosh with you. But you're like, forget that, I just got my nails done and my spray tan hasn't fully dried yet. The Bodyguard Jersey Shore is the perfect solution. It allows you to ward off unwanted advances at the clubs without physical harm, so the next day, when your tan is dry, you can hook up with that juicehead with no hard feelings."

Smith & Wesson spokespeople declined to offer details on exactly how the Bodyguard Jersey Shore works, but industry insiders speculate that the technology relies on remote steroid neutralization. "If you can make the guy's abs look really lame, you have the power and respect" stated J-Woww, an early adopter of the Bodyguard Jersey Shore Edition system. "It's like 'I own you now guido!' One more move and I'll show the whole club that you're a skank with no abs."

2010

New materials and manufacturing processes continue to revolutionize the gun and accessories industry. Blade-Tech, leading manufacturer of injection molded tactical holsters, announces availability of their next generation hybrid holsters.

The Blade-Tech Bacon Hybrid Holster blended the three most valuable elements in nature: leather, Kydex and bacon.

"Our new hybrid line combines what are the finest three materials known to man – kydex, leather, and bacon" bragged Blade-Tech CEO Ben Cartwright. "After we announced our new kydex / leather hybrid holsters earlier this year, we immediately started thinking about ways to reach the next level of defensive culinary performance."

One of the primary objectives of the new triple hybrid line was ease and speed of draw. Blade-Tech product managers tested thousands of materials before settling on bacon as the foundation of the new holster. Early customers agree with the choice and recognize distinct speed of draw advantages. "This new bacon holster is sure slick on the draw" gushed Clayton Moore, better known as The Lone Ranger. "I have to admit that the whole rig can get a little greasy at times, but on the plus side, it's a heck of a lot easier to put on my tight cowboy pants now."

Industry insiders were given advance looks at the new holster line. Roy Huntington, Editor of American Handgunner Magazine recently completed a comprehensive review of the new triple hybrid. "Mmmmmm. Bacon." purred Huntington.

Asked about future versions of the bacon holster, Cartwright replied "You might look for a double thick version in the near future. We think its a good way to consolidate a day's worth of emergency rations right in the holster itself."

2011

Ruger adds fuel to the fire of the pocket arms race with the announcement of the Ruger LCBM Pocket Rocket Pistol. Designed to offer maximum defensive power in a lightweight and pocket sized form factor, the LCBM retains many of the LC9 features while increasing payload. Like the LC9, the new LCBM offers double action only operation, a locked-breech design, and smooth trigger pull. However, contrary to the LC9 design, the new models will require customized holsters with liquid oxygen fueling apparatus.

"We're ending the small caliber gun debate once and for all" observed Ruger CEO Ben Cartwright. "The first LCBM models will carry a single .25 kiloton warhead, but we're working on subsequent models that will offer up to 6 +1 multiple re-entry bullets, or MIRB's. That should be enough gun to handle most imaginable self defense situations. Hopefully the LCBM will give new meaning to the phrase "come on punk, make my day.""

Introduced in 2011, the first Ruger LCBM pistol featured a .25 kiloton warhead.

Product managers at Ruger explain that the new Pocket Rocket technology simply became a matter of necessity. "We were working on .44 Magnum and .50 caliber LC prototypes, the LC44 and LC50 respectively, and quickly found that recoil in the seven ounce guns was just a little too stout, even for our experienced product testers like Harry Callahan" explained Ruger Product Manager Gene Kranz.

In a related announcement, Crimson Trace announced its next generation integral aiming units for the new LCBM. Similar to the existing LG-431 Front Activation Laserguard model, the unit is also custom designed for the LC series, but will now feature GPS aiming, instead of laser, technology. Early models will boast accuracy to within 100 feet, easily within the effective radius of the LCBM.

2013 and Beyond...

As we'll learn from "A Second Amendment Fairy Tale" in the next chapter, 2013 marked the year of the great gun freak-out. Manufacturers like Smith & Wesson, Ruger and Springfield Armory have dozens of new designs ready for production, but can't make enough of them. Factory lines are running 24x7 to meet the astronomical demand of consumers fearful of future gun bans and this leaves little production capacity for new designs. When the situation chillaxes a bit, and production capacity frees up a tad, we'll see a slew of new models hit the market.

CHAPTER 2 - Rules of Gun Safety

Buying a gun is a major responsibility - one that requires that you put absolute safety first and foremost in your plans. As you'll see by the four rules of gun safety outlined in this section, safety rules are often redundant - you have to break more than one for something to go wrong. Learn these rules. Make your friends and family learn them. Make sure every new shooter you take to the range understands these rules. And have fun!

"Carrying a gun is not "about the swagger." I own a lawnmower, too, but I don't fantasize about cutting the grass."

~ Mike Mollenhour, Frequent shooter, an everyday lawyer, an ex-soldier, and a soon-to-be-world famous author. He exercises the First Amendment about the Second Amendment, liberty, and national defense blogging at www.virtualmilitia.com

Rule 1

A gun is always loaded!

Yes. Always. Like Lindsay Lohan and the questions on *60 Minutes*. Even when it's not.

Every year we hear about people who are accidentally shot with 'unloaded' guns.

"I thought it was unloaded!"

"I'm sure I unloaded it last time I put it away!"

"It wasn't loaded before!"

"Maybe I was loaded last time I unloaded it!"

Of course, a gun is not technically always loaded. But the intent of Rule 1 is to **treat a gun as if it's always loaded**. If you treat a gun like it is loaded, you tend to change your behavior in terms of how you handle that gun.

Hopefully you won't check out the sights by aiming it at someone.

And of course you won't pull the trigger, unless you're actually ready to fire the gun at a safe target. More on that in a minute.

And certainly you won't do anything else careless with it.

Rule 1 is first on the priority list, because it's Rule 1, but also because it covers a lot of safety ground. Treating a gun like it is loaded and ready to fire has a fantastic ripple effect that makes everyone around safer.

So take it seriously. Pretend that a gun is loaded every single time you look at it or touch it. Pretty soon you'll start believing that it IS actually loaded. Even when you look, and verify that it's not, you'll want to look again to make sure. This is a good thing. Never ignore a gut feeling to check the status of a gun just one more time to be sure.

I like to have some fun with this when teaching new shooters the safety rules. Not for fun's sake alone, but to really drive home the point. Immediately after telling them Rule 1, the gun is always loaded, I pick up a gun, point it in a safe direction, and open gun's action to show them. It's empty of course, but I don't tell them that. I ask them if the gun is loaded. It's even better when both kids and adults are present in this new shooter orientation. Almost without fail, the kids look at me with an odd puzzled look for a second, then respond "Yes! It IS loaded!" Kids are much better students than adults. They love getting this trick question right! Adults tend to score about 50% on this pop quiz. About half of them cautiously inspect the gun, then tell me that the gun appears to be unloaded. We all have a quick laugh when I tell them, "WRONG! It's ALWAYS loaded!" Then they get it.

Is this obviously "empty" revolver loaded? YES! A gun is ALWAYS loaded!

So be creative when talking about the rules of gun safety with others. You can have fun teaching people to be safe - and just maybe they'll tend to remember a little better!

Rule 2

Keep your finger off the trigger until ready to fire!

Modern guns are pretty safe mechanical devices. While you should never rely on any mechanical device for safety - as anything can fail - it's really, really unlikely that a modern gun will fire without someone or something pressing its trigger. Most guns can be dropped or even thrown with no risk of firing. Others require one - or more - safety devices to be deactivated before a trigger pull will even allow the gun to fire. So more than likely, when you hear a story about a "gun just going off" you can generally assume that someone, somehow, moved that trigger.

All of these are reasons why Rule 2 is so important. It's nearly impossible for a modern gun to fire without someone or something pressing its trigger. If your finger is not on the trigger, it sure is hard to inadvertently press it!

Unless you're about to fire, keep your trigger finger placed like this. Not only is it safe, it let's others around you easily see that you're being safe.

Rule 2 might be the hardest habit for new shooters to cement in their memory.

It's a hook after all. That makes a perfect finger rest. You have opposable digits that are designed to grasp things. All of your available fingers prefer to move together in the same direction, so when the middle, ring and pinky finger close around a gun grip, the index finger wants to close also. The natural and instinctive motion when picking up a gun is to grasp it with your finger on the trigger.

It's a massive temptation. And a terribly unsafe habit that needs to be broken through practice and repetition. Scientists say that it takes 1,000 to 2,000 repetitions of an action to firmly establish an automatic habit in your brain. The same concept applies to learning how to keep your finger off the trigger.

It's fairly easy to train someone not to put their finger on the trigger when they pick up a gun. A few reminders generally solves that problem. But there is far more to developing really safe trigger discipline. It has to become an ingrained reflex no matter what the scenario. Immediately after their last shot, does that finger come off the trigger? When changing magazines, does the finger come off the trigger? Does the finger come off between the last shot and setting the gun back down on the table or putting it back in a holster? What if you have to move during the middle of shooting? Will your finger automatically come off the trigger? What about if you are interrupted or startled while shooting? Will your brain still remember to tell you finger to back off?

So training yourself, or others, to keep the finger off the trigger until ready to fire is a chore. Reminding someone over and over to get their finger off the trigger can ruffle some feathers. But you can make the training process respectful, un-intimidating and even fun. When taking new shooters to the range, I tell them (with a smile of course) that I'm going to have to remind them frequently to remove their trigger finger. With some discussion beforehand, no one gets defensive when you have to nudge them at the range. You can also have your family and friends train you. Just ask them to watch you shoot while focusing on your trigger finger.

Rule 3

Never point a gun at anything you're not willing to destroy!

Besides, pistol whipping can be a great alternative.

Nah, just kidding!

We like to keep things simple around here. You'll hear lots of terminology variations that describe rule 3.

"Never cover anything you're not willing to destroy!"

"Don't muzzle anything you're not prepared to shoot!"

"Always keep the gun pointed in a safe direction!"

"Never let the muzzle cover anything you're not willing to destroy!"

"Point the muzzle only at non-targets!"

While there are a number of ways to describe Rule 3, we like the direct approach. After all, not everyone understands the terminology of "covering." To a novice shooter, "covering" or "muzzling" could have meanings more related to group hugs than where a gun is pointed.

Muzzle

A muzzle is the fiery end of a gun. It's where the bullet comes out. It's the hole in the end that you never, ever, ever want to be looking at.

If you want to get technical, it's the front opening of a gun barrel. The barrel as a whole contains the rapidly burning propellant gases and guide the bullet on its path. Since we're talking about muzzles, it's a good time to mention the other end of the barrel. Located in the back, it is referred to as the breach. Breach, back. Muzzle, front. Simple right?

The key word in Rule 3 is NEVER. According to the Random House Dictionary, the word "never" has two definition components. Not ever or at no time. And to no extent or degree. The "to no extent or degree" part is actually the most important when considered with Rule 3.

It's fairly obvious that should not stand around and keep a gun pointed at someone or something that should not be shot. It's far less obvious to think about "pointing" as the act of allowing the muzzle to face someone or something for the briefest instant. It's still considered "pointing" if that muzzle simply moves across something you don't intend to shoot.

I like to tell shooters to think about the muzzle of a gun as a mega-powered, laser-beam, light saber of doom with no off button. Sort of like those big spotlights at used car dealerships. This destructive beam continues in (mostly) a straight line from the gun muzzle to infinity - and beyond. This beam waves around wherever the gun muzzle points - all the time. So if the muzzle "points" at something, even for a microsecond, that certain something is destroyed.

The muzzle beam of destruction is activated whenever you touch a gun. It doesn't matter if it's in a gun store, a show, at the range, in your home, or in a gun holster. When you touch it, the beam turns on and you have to watch every single movement for every single instant. As you move the gun around, what does that beam cross? Or, if you set a gun on the table to do something to it, where is it pointing? I see this scenario at the range all the time. If there is a malfunction, people will set the gun down to work on it, not realizing it's pointed at the shooter next to them.

It may sound obvious as you read this, but Rule 3 includes your own body and extremities - not just those of others. Consider where the muzzle points as you pick up a gun, inspect it, put it away, draw it from a holster or whatever. Be especially cautious of muzzling your arm or leg as they tend to move around and have a great probability of being in the wrong place at the wrong time!

Rule 4

Be sure of your target and what's behind it!

Because impersonating the Los Angeles Police Department is a crime!

But seriously, bullets tend to go through things. That's one of the reason they are so good at being bullets.

So the key part of Rule 4 is the "what's behind it" part. There are two reasons that you need to carefully consider what's behind the target.

First, your bullet may go right through the target and continue out the back, still traveling at great velocity. If it's still moving after passing through the first target, it's still dangerous.

Second, unlike James Bond and The Lone Ranger, it's possible for us mortals to miss the primary target once in a while. And if you miss, there is a zero percent chance that your target will stop your bullet.

The bullets on the left passed right through stone floor tile with enough energy left over to plow 10 inches deep into wet newspaper.

Rule 4 uses the words "be sure" for a very good reason. Unless you are absolutely positive about what's behind your target, don't shoot. Being "pretty sure" isn't good enough when it comes to gun safety. If your view is obscured, don't shoot. Be positive.

CHAPTER 3 - Types of Guns

Handguns

We're not going to get wrapped up too much in the specifics of proper gun terminology. It can be intimidating and quite frankly, it's not all that important as long as people know what you're trying to say. But we will try to be accurate most of the time so you have the full picture.

Right off the bat, we're going to run into a problematic situation. You see, some gun folks are so darn persnickety about using the correct words that someone, somewhere, is bound to correct you on your use of a gun word. Maybe you'll walk into a gun store and ask if they carry extra clips for your Springfield XD handgun. Or perhaps you'll refer to your Smith & Wesson 642 Airweight as a "pistol". Do they know what you mean? Yes. Is it really necessary to cop an attitude and correct you? No.

Here's one way to deal with that kind of thing should you walk into a gun store and get the terminology treatment…

You: Hi! I have a question…

Surly Gun Store Clerk: (Ignores you and continues talking to the gun shop groupies behind the counter)

You: Ummm, hello! I was wondering if you could help me out?

Clerk: Yeah, what?

You: I need to see if you have some extra clips for my new Glock.

Clerk: (Slowly turns to friends and does a full-body eye roll…) No, sorry, we don't.

You: Aren't these Glock clips here in the display case?

Clerk: Nope, those are magazines.

You: Well, do you have any that fit a Glock 17?

Clerk: Yeah.

You: Bless your heart… Now will you be a dear and sell me some of those MAGAZINES?

See what you did there? Here in the south, the phrase "bless your heart" loosely translates into something along the lines of "you're really a clueless jerk, aren't you?" The beauty is that you can say it with a bit of an accent and dripping with more sweetness than an extra large Chick-Fil-A iced tea. It's a beautiful solution to many of life's challenges. While we're on magazines, let's define "magazine" and "clip."

Magazines and Clips

You know how you can spot a high school prom couple at an exclusive restaurant? Like when the pimply mannish boy requests A-1 Steak Sauce with his Chateaubriand? Well, there's a similar thing in shooting – when people carelessly throw around words like clip.

Clips and magazines are both legitimate shooting related objects. While sometimes subtle, there are differences.

A clip is a device used to hold cartridges for the purpose of storage, packing, and easy loading into a magazine. Clips were a big deal back when the world had anger issues expressed by frequent large-scale wars. Five or ten rounds of ammo might be attached to a clip, which would allow a soldier to slide the rounds into the magazine of his rifle or handgun quickly and easily. Clips are still used today. Some .223 or 5.56 ammunition comes on clips to make it easier to load lots of rounds into a magazine at once.

A magazine is the container that holds cartridges for the purpose of feeding them into the chamber of a firearm. Magazines can be built into the gun, as with many rifles, or they can be removable, as with most semi-automatic pistols and AR type rifles. That thing that falls out the bottom of a Glock? That's a magazine.

Confused? No problem. We've got a near fail-safe tip for you. These days you're pretty safe referring to most things that hold bullets as a magazine. More often than not, you'll be correct referring to it that way.

While the shooting industry is starting to get pretty good at traditional retail things like civility and customer service, you'll still run into the occasional Clems who might look down their nose at new shooters. Ignore them and move on. Because you'll find that, overwhelmingly, the shooting community is full of really nice and respectable folks that want to help. Try us on this. Go to a big match to watch. And you'll see things like the industry's most famous professionals stop to ask if you need help. Other shooters will ask if you need to borrow a gun or ammunition. 95% of the youth in attendance will refer to you as "maam" or "sir."

So don't get hung up on exact terminology. And by all means, don't let that be a barrier to your participation! We know what you mean after all!

With all that said, we're going to point out correct terminology for specific things in this book, just so you know, but don't get too worked up about it. Shooting sports are supposed to be fun after all.

In this book, we're going to refer to handguns as any type of hand-held firearm. Handguns can be one of many types - semi-automatic pistols, revolvers, derringers or single shot models. Next, we'll talk about some of those in a bit more detail.

Pistols

If we get really nitpicky, we would define "pistol" as a handgun that has it's chamber integral with the barrel.

Chamber

You can think of the chamber of a gun as the very back part of the barrel, where a cartridge is placed and ready to fire. As with all this complicated gun stuff, a chamber is not always the same as the back of the barrel. Revolvers have chambers that are separate from the barrel. They still hold the cartridge in place to fire, however, revolver chambers line up with the back of the barrel when ready to fire.

Note how revolver chambers (left) are not attached to the barrel. With the semi-automatic (right), the chamber is part of the barrel.

So technically, a pistol could be a single shot pistol, a derringer or perhaps a semi-automatic pistol like these two Berettas.

Here are two semi-automatic pistols. On the left, a Beretta Tomcat, and on the right, a Beretta 92FS.

For purposes of this book, we're going to use the word pistol primarily to describe semi-automatic pistols like the ones shown above. If we talk about other types of pistols, like single shots and derringers, we'll be sure to specify.

We've mentioned "semi-automatic pistols" a couple of times so far, so we ought to spend just a second specifying what those are. Semi-automatic simply indicates that the gun does part of the work for you. It's not fully automatic, meaning that it doesn't shoot multiple times with one pull of the trigger. Get it? Semi as in "part," and automatic as in "you don't have to do all the work."

Many guns use some of the energy from a firing cartridge to eject the empty cartridge shell and load a new one for you. The "semi" part of semi-automatic is important here because you, the shooter, still have to operate the gun. When you pull the trigger, it only fires one time and one time only. All that's automated is ejection of the spent cartridge case and loading of the next cartridge into the chamber. You can think of a semi-automatic handgun design kind of like of like an electric staple gun. You have to press the go switch to staple something, it just gets it ready to go for you. Or you could think of semi-automatic kind of like politicians and TV cameras. When you make a deliberate action to turn on a TV camera, a politician will automatically reload right in front of it.

Most semi-automatic pistols are pretty similar at first glance. Modern ones generally have a magazine in the grip that holds the cartridges and prepares them for loading into the chamber. So, unlike a revolver, a pistol arranges extra cartridges vertically. As the gun is fired, a spring in the magazine pushes the stack of cartridges upwards towards the chamber.

Folks who favor semi-automatic pistols like them for many reasons.

- Semi-automatic pistols generally have more cartridge capacity than revolvers. This simply means they hold more bullets and you don't have to reload it as often. Many modern pistols can hold up to 20 cartridges in the magazine.

- Pistols are easier and faster to reload than revolvers. To reload a pistol, the user simply activates a button or lever to release the empty magazine. Then you insert a full one.

- Semi-automatic pistols may appear to have less recoil - all else being equal. While physics is physics and the overall recoil force is the same, some of the recoil energy is directed towards the semi-automatic operation of the pistol. So many shooters report "feeling" less recoil with a semi-automatic pistol than a comparably powered revolver.

If you talk to a couple of gun aficionados, you're likely to hear about what sounds like yet another type of handgun - the 1911. No worries, it's just a type of semi-automatic pistol. People tend to get pretty passionate about 1911 style pistols so they tend to get placed in their own category.

1911

You'll hear gun folks talk in reverential tones about something called a 1911. Yes, it's a year. It also sounds a little bit like a famous model of Porsche. But in context of this book, it's a pistol design. Not a manufacturer or a specific model, but a design. Kind of like how a pickup truck is a design. Lot's of car manufacturers make them, and you can get them with different size engines, but they all have some common features, like seats in the front and a cargo bed in the back.

Here's a 1911 model pistol made by Springfield Armory. It's the TRP Armory Kote model.

It's not a perfect analogy, but 1911's are kind of like pickup trucks. They are all based on a semi-automatic pistol design, invented and brought to market in, you guessed it, the year 1911 by one John Moses Browning. 1911's have a number of common design elements, regardless of which manufacturer makes them and often parts are interchangeable. For example, classic 1911's are all single-action semi-automatics, have a thumb and grip safety, and a similar design to lock and unlock the barrel during recoil.

1911's have a lot to live up to. They have been known to take down both a Japanese Zero fighter and German Storch observation plane in World War II. In fact, some believe that a stray 1911 .45 ACP round inadvertently destroyed the city of Dresden. OK, the Dresden thing may be a slight exaggeration, but the 1911 has been a phenomenally successful and long-lived design.

There are different types of semi-automatic pistols, and since you'll hear about some of these at gun stores, shows and ranges, we'll take a look at three major types later in this chapter: single-action, double-action and striker-fired.

Revolvers

Revolvers are easy to master from a terminology standpoint.

According to the Urban Dictionary, Revolver is the Beatles greatest album and was released in 1966. That doesn't really help much unless you're learning to shoot with Sgt. Pepper's Lonely Hearts Club Band. So we can turn to Dictionary.com and see that the verb revolve means to turn around or rotate, as on an axis. That's more helpful!

A pair of Ruger revolvers. The Super Blackhawk (above) is a single-action. The LCR .357 (below) is a double-action.

All revolvers have multiple chambers arranged in a cylinder. The cylinder rotates in order to line up each chamber with the barrel when it's ready to fire. Simple right? If you see a handgun that has a round cylinder, you've got an excellent chance of identifying it correctly as a revolver!

Some folks prefer revolvers because they are simple and reliable.

• As the chambers are all in the cylinder, it's very easy to check if a revolver is loaded or unloaded. But remember, a gun is always loaded!

• Double-action revolvers are simple to operate. Just pull the trigger and it will fire. There are no external safeties or magazine operations to worry about.

• A single-action revolver is a great gun for new shooters as it's very deliberate. To fire a shot, you have to first cock the hammer, then pull the trigger.

• While there are exceptions, most revolvers can hold between 5 and 8 cartridges in a cylinder. Some small caliber revolvers can hold more than 8.

Caliber [kal-uh-ber]

- Noun

1. The interior diameter of the bore of a gun barrel, usually measured in inches or millimeters.

A gun barrel with an interior diameter of .357 inches in diameter is technically .357 caliber. Caliber measures the diameter of the bullet and has nothing to do with length or weight of the actual bullet, although calibers have taken on broader meaning in casual conversation. If someone refers to a caliber of 9mm, then they are really talking about a 9mm Luger cartridge and all the assumptions that go with that.

2. A sinister plot by gun people to make things extra-confusing for new shooters.

For example, .38 caliber really means .357 inches in diameter and .380 caliber really means .355 inches in diameter. 9 millimeter also means .355 inches in diameter. To keep things plenty confusing, .40 caliber really does mean .40 inches in diameter. Same with .45 caliber - that means .45 inches. However, .44 caliber really means .430 inches. Of course, .32 ACP (caliber) really means .312 inches. .30 caliber rifle bullets are particularly easy. Some are .308 inches and others are .311 inches. Got it? See, isn't this gun stuff easy?

In a minute, we'll talk about two types of revolvers, double-action and single-action.

Derringers

Even though the word "derringer" sounds French, it still manages to sound tough doesn't it?

Technically, a derringer is a pocket pistol, and for any given caliber, it's about as small a gun as you can get. Derringers typically are designed to fire single shots and are very simple mechanically. This simplicity allows them to be very small.

Original derringers were single shot muzzle loaders - you know, like the pistols in Pirates of the Caribbean, only much, much smaller. Modern derringers tend to have two barrels, with each loaded with a single cartridge. Even though many modern derringers can fire two shots, it's not because they have a repeating action. They just have two single shot barrels duct taped together. Well, only the really cheap ones are duct taped. Higher quality models use staples. Nah, still kidding. Modern derringers are actually really nice guns that are the pocket gun equivalent of a nice over and under shotgun with two barrels carefully machined or welded together.

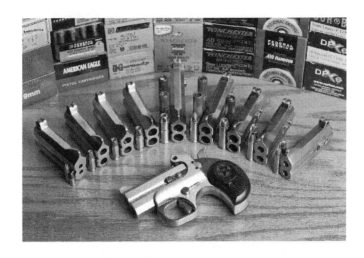

Bond Arms makes outstanding modern derringers. Bond models allow you to config-ure multiple caliber and barrel options on the same gun frame. Image: Rick Arnold / BGilCommunications.com

The Bond Arms double-barrel pistol is more than just another derringer. Its modular grip and barrel system allow shooters to take advantage of a wide variety of pistol and .410 cartridges. All of the components I put to the test exceeded my expectations for quality and performance.

~ B. Gil Horman, Freelance Writer, NRA American Rifleman Contributor and all around swell guy. www.bgilcommunications.com

Because the history of derringers is such as fascinating tale, we're going to take a quick diversion here.

A Brief History of The Derringer

Coincidentally, the derringer pistol was invented by an American gunsmith named Henry Deringer. Yes, that's Deringer with one "r." Imagine the odds of that! But back to the story. Deringer ran a thriving business in Philadelphia, manufacturing Model 1814 and 1817 Common Rifles for military contracts. Of course, the real cash cow for Deringer's business was running guided tours of Rocky V film locations.

Back to guns. Deringer was famous for his small pistol designs, which were all single shot muzzle loaders, usually of large-caliber. In

1852, he started making the pistols pocket-sized and they became known as derringers - with two "R's." Why the public added that second "R" remains a mystery.

Henry Deringer did not think of his derringer pistol as anything particularly noteworthy and therefore never patented his invention. Seeing market opportunity, Apple quickly launched the iDerringer to capitalize on the design's popularity. As a result, Henry died leaving only a modest estate and was never invited to ring the opening bell at the New York Stock Exchange.

As the derringer gained in popularity, specific designs for women, called muff pistols, became fashionable. No, we're not making this up. Muff pistols were popular as the small derringer could easily fit in hand muffs, thereby offering concealment and quick access should an urgent self-defense need arise.

After President Lincoln was assassinated by a bad actor, John Wilkes Booth, with a Philadelphia Derringer in 1865, Henry Deringer was overcome with anguish. Leaving the life of guns behind, he decided to change not only his name, but his life's work. Adding another "R" to his last name, and assuming the first name of "Rick", Derringer was confident this bold new identity change would hide his past. Now known as Rick Derringer, he helped form a pop band called The McCoys and played lead guitar and a little bass on occasion. Success came slowly for Derringer and The McCoys and they released their first hit in 1965 - a single titled Hang on Sloopy. At the age of 179 Derringer had managed to reinvent his life. Hang on Sloopy paid homage to the importance of small, personal defense weapons as the song tells the story of Sloopy, who lived in a very bad part of town, where everybody tried to put her down. Many also put down her daddy, but Derringer didn't care what her daddy do.

Rick Derringer continued to drift away from his gun-making past and launched another hit single in the 1970's titled Rock and Roll, Hoochie Koo. However, Derringer's songwriting continued to drop hints of his more tactical past with lyrics like "lawdy mama, light my fuse."

During Rick Derringer's absence from the gun industry, derringer pistols declined in popularity. The advent of small revolvers and even smaller semi-automatic pistols diminished the advantages of one or two shot derringers.

Until the advent of Cowboy Action Shooting that is…

In 1995, Greg Bond, custom derringer maker and half-brother James, officially founded Bond Arms. Never one to enjoy tuxedos and that silly accent, Greg parted ways with his brother and headed west across the pond to Granbury, Texas. Insistent on his belief that modern gun design could be applied to the derringer, Bond brought several innovations to the classic derringer design. In addition to easy locking double barrels and a safer rebounding hammer design, Bond introduced the idea of interchangeable barrels. Now, one derringer frame could use barrels from the lowly .22 long rifle all the way up to .45 Colt. Even when pressed, Bond would not comment on rumors of his brother's custom 40mm grenade derringer.

Continuing to distance himself from the family spy business, Bond and his Arms became ingrained in the Cowboy Action Shooting competition circuit where models like the Snake Slayer helped good guys and villains alike win 10 consecutive titles.

Derringers continue to be popular today, where they are a mainstay fixture on the World Poker Tour - except of course in the City of New York, where the King has banned playing cards.

"Every example you can come up with in which a derringer would be ideal, I can come up with another gun that would do the job that much better."

~ T. Michael Hast, Shooting Aficianado and Customer Holster Maker Extraordinaire, www.theholstersite.com

Single Shot

We're not going to spend a lot of time on single-shot handguns as the name pretty much sums things up.

Single-shot handguns fire once.

Then you have to reload them.

Modern single-shot handguns are generally used for hunting and firing unusual calibers. Like the modern derringer, many feature interchangeable barrels. You might hear of "Thompson Center" handguns. These are a great example of a modern single shot handgun. The action breaks open so that the chamber is exposed. This allows loading of a single cartridge.

The Thompson Center G2 Contender is a great example of a modern single-shot handgun.

Handgun Action!

While we're here defining handguns, we need to find some action.

We've already covered TYPES of handguns (like pistols and revolvers) but now we need to talk for a minute about types of action. And when I say "action" I'm talking about the method of operation of that handgun.

It gets a bit complicated as both pistols and revolvers can have the same type of action.

• You can have a single-action revolver.

• You can also have a single-action pistol.

• You can have a double-action pistol OR revolver.

• But you can't have a striker-fired revolver. That I know of.

Let's talk about action types for a minute. Once you see what they are, a lot of the mystery will simply evaporate. Like BTU's from Al Gore's mansion.

Single-Action

Single-action is a pretty simple concept. And it has nothing to do with online dating sites, chance encounters at the laundromat or a night on the town with two wild and crazy guys.

When a handgun is single-action, whether it's a pistol or revolver, it does one thing, or action, when you pull the trigger. The descriptor, single-action, must be entirely coincidental right?

While I'm sure there's an exception out there, in most cases, pressing the trigger of a single-action gun will release a hammer or striking contraption of sorts, allowing it to strike a firing pin that whacks the back of a cartridge and ignites it. So, pressing the trigger does one action - which results in firing the gun.

These are both single-action handguns. Note the hammers in the cocked position. The trigger just releases the hammer.

Here's where it gets tricky. Some single-action guns need to be manually cocked between each shot. Perhaps the best example of this is the traditional cowboy six gun, or single-action revolver. The shooter must "cock the hammer" to prepare it for the single-action release by a trigger press. In old western movies, this is done really fast - sometimes with the shooter smacking the hammer with one hand while holding the trigger down with the other.

Hammer [ham-er]

1. The part of a firearm designed to provide energy to the firing pin in order to strike the primer of a cartridge. Some hammers, such as those on older revolvers, have the firing pin attached to the hammer and directly impact the primer. Others, generally on more modern designs, impact a transfer bar or mechanism to provide energy to the firing pin. The hammer of a gun does not have to be exposed or visible. For example, the Smith and Wesson 642 revolver and M1 Garand semi-automatic rifle both have internal hammers.

2. Easily confused with similar terms. For example, Hammer Time is not an appropriate usage in the context of guns. Unless you got slick moves and a pair of parachute pants capable of providing wind power for San Francisco or maybe smuggling dozens of illegal immigrants across the border. Otherwise, you can't touch this.

Important Safety Tip: While it's OK to cock your hammer, don't ever hammer your... Ummm. Never mind.

Here's a great example of a single-action handgun - a Ruger Vaquero. Cock the hammer. Pull the trigger. Repeat. Image: Sturm, Ruger & Co.

However, just because a gun is single-action does not mean it has to be manually cocked between each shot. Some single-action designs, like the 1911 pistol, are cocked for the first shot. Each subsequent shot uses the recoil action to automatically cock the hammer for the next shot. Since the trigger still does only one thing, release the hammer, these guns are still considered single-actions.

So what's the big deal about single action?

Generally speaking - again, I'll bet a nickel someone will find an exception - single-action guns have relatively light triggers since the trigger only serves to release the hammer. That doesn't take a lot of pressure. A light trigger pull makes for a gun that is easier to shoot accurately. It's not technically more accurate, just easier to shoot accurately. This is because the force of your finger is less likely to pull the sights off target. If it takes 8 pounds of pressure to press the trigger, and the gun only weighs 2 pounds, then the shooter really has to concentrate to keep that gun perfectly still during a trigger press. On the other hand, if the trigger press requires 2 pounds, and the gun weighs 3 pounds, then the shooter is less likely to pull the gun off target while pressing the trigger.

So, all of that is a fancy way of saying that many folks like single-action guns because they can be easy to shoot accurately.

There's a lot more to consider when deciding whether to use a single-action gun, so for now, let's just stick to the definitions. We'll talk about pros and cons later in the book.

Double-Action

Double-action is not a dirty word, so get that out of your head.

Double-action simply means that the trigger press motion can accomplish not one, but two, distinct actions. A double action gun can use the trigger press to both cock the gun and release the hammer or striker to fire it. So, with a double-action gun, you don't (necessarily) need to cock the hammer in order to fire the gun. A trigger press can accomplish both actions.

By necessity, and those pesky laws of physics (Dang that Newton guy!), a double-action gun requires more force to operate the trigger. That's because the trigger is cocking and releasing the hammer or striker. It does more work, so it requires more energy on your part. There's no such thing as a free lunch.

Here's the part where we start talking about complications and exceptions. You knew that was coming right?

One of the benefits of most double-action guns is that they can operate in either double-action or single-action mode. Technically, you could refer to these as DA/SA (double-action/single-action) guns. For purposes of simplicity, we'll just call them double-action. Just be aware there are some double-action pistols that have no single-action mode.

Both of these are double-action handguns. A Beretta PX4 Storm .40 S&W caliber (above) and a Ruger LCR .357 revolver (below)

To illustrate this point, lets look at a really common double-action pistol - the Beretta 92FS. This is the civilian version of the standard pistol that United States military men and women use.

The Beretta 92FS is a classic double-action pistol design. Once a cartridge is loaded in the chamber, there are two ways to fire the pistol. Method one is to simply pull the trigger, making sure the safety lever is off first. You'll notice that the trigger requires a longer press, with more pressure, to fire the shot. That's because as you press the trigger, the hammer is raised into the firing position. As you continue to press the trigger, the hammer is released, and the shot is fired.

Things get interesting after the first shot. Most double-action pistols (not revolvers) use some of the recoil energy from each shot to eject the spent cartridge casing, load a new cartridge and most importantly to this discussion, cock the hammer or striker. So, for subsequent shots, the pistol operates in single-action mode. Got that? The hammer is already cocked, so pressing the trigger does one thing (single-action) and that is releasing the hammer to fire the cartridge.

This Beretta 92 is a great example of a double-action pistol. The first press of the trigger cocks the hammer AND releases the sear to fire. Each subsequent shot operates in single-action with a lighter trigger press.

To sum it up, with double-action pistols, the first shot requires a longer, more forceful, trigger press to operate in double-action mode. Each subsequent shot operates in single-action with a a shorter and lighter trigger press since the hammer is cocked automatically.

Revolvers with exposed hammers work a little bit differently. You can press the trigger in double-action mode to cock the hammer and release it to fire the shot. You can also manually cock the hammer and fire the revolver in single-action mode. The difference lies in how the subsequent shots operate. With a double-action pistol, recoil energy is used to eject a spent cartridge, load a new one and cock the hammer. Revolvers have none of this. So, with the second shot with a revolver, the shooter is faced with a choice to shoot double-action again, or to manually cock the hammer and shoot single-action.

Some double-action revolvers do not have an exposed hammer, like the Ruger LCR shown here.

Since there is no way to manually cock the hammer, each shot is fired in double-action mode.

Some revolvers, like this Ruger LCR, do not have an exposed hammer. The only way to operate this one is in double-action mode. Each trigger press cocks the internal hammer and releases it to fire the shot.

So what's the big deal with double-action pistols?

The advantage of the double-action design is safety. Since the first trigger press requires a forceful and deliberate effort to cock the hammer and fire the gun, the shooter really has to intend to fire. An accidental finger twitch is less likely to result in a shot. There's some merit to the idea that in a high-stress situation like self-defense or law enforcement duties you don't want a trigger that's too easy to activate.

The primary disadvantage is the difference in feel between first and second shots. With double-action / single-action pistols, the first shot will require a longer and hard trigger press. Subsequent shots will require a lighter and shorter press. Acclimating a shooter to account for the difference, under stress, requires training.

So what do you do?

Try it for yourself. My collection has both single-action and double-action pistols and revolvers. I personally don't mind shooting double-action pistols like the Beretta 92. But then again, I like to shoot frequently and I practice. If you are realistically not going to practice on a regular basis, you may want to consider a design with fewer variables like a double-action only revolver or striker-fired pistol. We'll talk about those next.

Striker-Fired

Striker-fired pistols are a little ambiguous, and just to muddy the waters, there's a lot of confusion between which pistols are double-action, single-action and striker-fired. Some double-action / single-action pistols technically use a striker instead of a hammer. For purposes of simplicity - you're not believing the whole guns and simplicity thing are you? - we'll neglect those as we define striker-fired guns here.

First, let's define what striker-fired means, more or less.

While there will be more exceptions than visitors to a Jersey Shore spray tan salon, we'll refer to striker-fired guns as those with existing tension on the striker bar. Think of it this way. In a hammer fired gun, there may be a spring between the striker or firing pin and the cartridge. This spring prevents the striker or firing pin from hitting the cartridge until some external force, like a hammer, overcomes the pressure of the spring and forces the striker to hit the cartridge primer. In a striker-fired gun, the spring could be BEHIND the striker or firing pin. This means that constant pressure is being applied to the striker, encouraging it to move towards the cartridge primer and fire the gun. A sear prevents this motion until the trigger is pressed. A sear is simply a piece of metal that holds the hammer or striker in place until enough pressure if applied to the trigger.

Does that makes sense? In a double-action or single action scenario (generally speaking) there is pressure keeping the striker or firing pin separated from the live cartridge until a hammer is released to overcome that pressure. In a striker-fired situation, there is constant pressure on the striker towards the cartridge. The sear prevents the striker from releasing until the trigger is pressed.

A pair of Glocks - both striker-fired pistols.

If we were to get into the gory details, there's a bit more to the story. For example, most striker-fired guns maintain the striker in "partially" ready position. The trigger pull applies the rest of the tension necessary to complete a strike on the cartridge primer. This is one of the reasons that the lines between single, double-action and striker-fired designs are so blurry, but that's not relevant to our discussion here, so we'll move on.

This discussion of fire-control system engineering is all good and nice, but how is it relevant to choosing a gun that's right for you? Let's look at some real world pros and cons of striker-fired designs versus single and double-action designs.

So what's the big deal about striker-fired pistols?

Generally, striker-fired pistols offer a constant trigger pull from first to last shot. If you've been paying attention to all this mumbo-jumbo, you know that you can achieve constant, first to last shot, trigger pull with a double-action gun. Aha! You're right! But with a striker-fired gun, some of the pressure required to strike the firing pin exists before you start to pull the trigger. This means that a striker-fired gun can have a lighter trigger pull than a double-action gun, yet still offer the same pull weight for all shots. With a double-action gun, the trigger pull provides all the force required to cock the gun and fire it. With a striker-fired gun, the gun is partially cocked with the initial act of chambering a cartridge. Each subsequent shot also partially cocks the gun. So the trigger pull simply completed the cocking process, then releases the firing pin.

So the net-net of all this technical discussion? A striker-fired gun "acts" like a double-action gun where each trigger pull is the same. It also has a heavier trigger pull than a single-action gun, which provides more margin of safety against unintended discharges. But it's a lot easier to shoot well than a double-action gun with a heavy trigger pull.

What does a striker-fired handgun look like? A Glock.

Of course, many other modern pistols are striker-fired. Like the Smith & Wesson M&P and the Springfield Armory XD. There are lots of others of course. The point is that striker-fired guns have become insanely popular for the reasons stated here. When was the last time you saw a law enforcement officer of any type? The odds are 86.327% in favor of them carrying a striker-fired gun.

Enough about handgun action types. That stuff is exhausting.

Rifles

This is the Insanely PRACTICAL Guide to Guns and Shooting, so we're not going to get wrapped up in obscure technical differences between rifles and smoothbores. After all, the objective is to communicate information you need to know in order to survive and thrive a visit to a gun store, range or shooting club.

With that said, we're going to use two defining characteristics to explain what a rifle is.

First, a rifle is not a handgun. It's longer. And a rifle is generally intended to be fired using both hands and a shoulder for support. For obvious reasons, many people refer to rifles as long guns. Yes, really. Gun stuff is not always overly complex.

Second, a rifle has rifling. I know, that sounds like an epiphany from the Psychic Hotline. But it's true.

Rifling

Simply put, rifling refers to the interior shape of a gun barrel. Through a variety of techniques, grooves are cut or pressed into the metal interior of the barrel. These grooves are shaped in a spiral pattern, like those DNA strand pictures you saw in high school chemistry. With its rifling grooves, a gun barrel is just a gnats hair smaller in diameter than the bullet that it is intended to fire. So as a bullet is forced through the barrel, the rifling grabs the bullet and imparts spin. The whole idea behind this is for guns to be more impressive - like John Elway. When John Elway threw a pass, he gripped the football tightly and spun the ball as he threw. Not only does a ball fly with more stability and accuracy while spinning, the motion also keeps one of the pointy ends facing forward, so it flies farther and faster. In contrast, imagine John Elway throwing a football while wearing a baseball glove.

He can apply the same amount of force, but his passes wouldn't be helping his Hall of Fame aspirations. That might resemble trying to throw a live turkey.

Here's an example of a modern rifle. This one is a Ruger 10/22 that we customized to benefit Soldier's Angels Project Valour-IT. A lucky bidder now has a nice rifle and supported a great cause.

Rifles come in all shapes and sizes for different purposes. You can even buy them at many Wal-Mart's as they are common tools for hunting, home defense and recreation. Mostly, they vary by the type of action they use. Some common types include semi-automatic, lever-action, bolt-action, single-shot and pump-action. We'll talk about some of these later in the book.

A pair of evil "assault weapons?" Nah. Just rifles. We'll talk about the whole "assault weapon" myth next.

SHOOTING Myth!

Myth: Assault Weapons

There's no such thing as an "assault weapon." Next topic.

Oh, OK. There IS such a thing as an Assault Rifle. That specific term generally refers to a military rifle that is capable of firing in full-automatic mode. That is, it will keep shooting as long as the trigger is held down, until it runs out of ammunition. Ever see the movie Predator? Most of the guns in the movie ARE actually assault rifles - not assault weapons!

There's a lot of confusion, misunderstanding, and downright lies about assault weapons, so I hope to clarify this once and for all.

Assault Weapons are sneaky little morphing cretins. They have a unique ability to change their DNA day to day, hour to hour and again between the 6pm and 11pm news broadcasts. Just ask Dan Rather. Usually the cause of the metamorphosis can be traced back to political agenda, but sometimes T.V. personalities can cause shape shifting simply by their spoken word and some creative video editing.

While most people think the whole assault weapon panic is new, it's not. It dates back more than dozens of years.

Evidence of the first assault weapon was found at the Tamerza and Midés excavation site in Tunisia. Ancient writings offer evidence that an elitist Cro-Magnon Herald staff reporter filed reports accusing citizen Grog of possession of a rapid fire assault weapon, later to become known as a brick. Evidence suggests that Grog was known to carry two, and sometimes three bricks at a time – which many deemed excessive for sporting purposes.

During the middle ages, assault weapons became more sophisticated. Henry VIII was known to have, and frequently use, an assault divorce attorney.

Meanwhile, across the English Channel, Marie Antoinette was assaulted as a result of her secret possession of several pieces of assault cake.

Assault weapons continue to be heavily regulated. In most states, Rosie O'Donnell is classified as an assault weapon. Ownership generally requires the buyer to provide proof that they are legally deaf. This is a safety precaution that prevents Assault Rosie owners from going postal as a side effect of continuous exposure to re-runs of The View.

Many United States Marine Corps recruits view their drill instructors as assault weapons until, through the miracle of osmosis, they become assault weapons themselves. Many point to this phenomenon as proof of the redeeming societal value of assault weapons.

The primary differentiator between assault weapons and regular ole' weapons is that assault weapons are automatic, meaning they are known to automatically commit crimes, scare politicians from California, New York, and Massachusetts, and start world wars.

As assault weapons have spread throughout the world, they have evolved according to local environments. In the United States, most assault weapons are actually guns, with the exception of Assault Rosie of course. In the United Kingdom, assault weapons have taken the form of bread knives and cricket bats. Similarly, in France, most assault weapons are recognizable as three day old baguettes with a wheel of dried up brie, while Australia has battled proliferation of assault knives, assault swords, and most recently assault laser pointers.

Doesn't make much sense does it? That's exactly the outcome desired by proponents of the term "assault weapon."

Remember, this is such thing as an assault rifle. That's a real military gun that fires in fully automatic mode. There is not such thing as an assault weapon. That's a political myth engineered to confuse people.

Shotguns

As you're probably already figuring out, guns and their related terminology are intended to be understood only by wayward monks strung out on peyote. So recognizing that anything in the world of guns and shooting has exceptions, let's take a crack at a simple definition of a shotgun.

A shotgun has two primary characteristics. Mostly.

First, they fire "shells" that contain multiple spherical projectiles.

Second, unlike handguns and rifles, they have smooth, not rifled barrels.

Shotguns comes in all types. From top to bottom: A Browning BPS pump-action 12 gauge, a Browning Gold Fusion semi-automatic 12 gauge and a Winchester 9410 .410 lever-action.

While some companies make handguns that fire smaller shotgun shells, most shotguns are intended to be shoulder-fired. So at first glance, they resemble rifles. However, since they fire multiple projectiles with each shot, they tend to be better suited for hitting close-range moving objects - like birds or clay targets. The interior of a shotgun barrel is (generally) not rifled as rifling would impart spin on the column of pellets as they move down the barrel and this would cause the pellets to disperse too widely upon leaving the muzzle.

Throwing Rocks

Shotgun ammunition (except slugs which we'll talk about later in the book) is generally composed of multiple projectiles in a single cartridge - or shell if you want to be technical. Here's an easy way to visualize how shotguns work. Imagine chunking a rock at a squirrel that keeps raiding your bird feeder. If you throw one rock at that gluttonous little bugger, that's kinda like using a "normal" handgun or rifle. You have to aim that single rock pretty carefully. But on the plus side, you can throw it pretty far as all of your arm strength is focused on that one rock. If you pick up a handful of rocks, and throw them all at once, that's kind of like a shotgun. You might stand a little better chance of hitting your irreverent squirrel at short distances, but he's not going to be quite as aggravated as if he was bonked with a single, well-aimed rock. That's because your throwing strength is spread out across all the rocks. Each one get's a fraction of the power generated by your bicep and tricep guns. Make sense?

Shotgun shells can contain "shot" or single projectiles called slugs. Left to right: 12 gauge slug, 12 gauge 00 buckshot, 12 gauge 7 ½ shot and a .410 shotshell with 7 ½ size shot.

The shot (or rocks in our example) in a shotgun shell can consist of some number of lead or steel pellets. Some shotgun shells, like buckshot, have a small number of pellets like 8 to 15 depending on the specific shell. These buckshot pellets can be up to ⅓ of an inch in diameter. These are typically used for self defense or hunting larger game. Ouch! Other shotgun shells designed for hitting fast moving clay targets or birds and might have hundreds of small pellets in each shell. While more pellets offer a greater chance of hitting the target, they are light in weight and lose energy quickly.

So the basic tradeoff with shotguns when compared to rifles is multiple projectiles versus distance. A shotgun is a great tool for hitting targets at close range, like 50 yards or less, while a rifle is great for hitting targets at longer range.

Even though a shotgun fires multiple projectiles, you still have to aim it.

Speaking of Aiming, We Aim to Confuse!

Shotguns and shotgun ammunition was designed with one primary objective - to completely confuse the uninitiated!

Here's why.

Like other guns, shotguns come in different sizes, where the size really refers to the diameter of the barrel. While handguns and rifles use caliber to indicate their relative size, shotguns have their own system. The inventor of the shotgun naming convention must have been that kid who always raised their hand first in elementary school. You see, most shotguns are measured and named by gauge. Not a gauge. Just gauge. You've probably heard of 12 gauge or 20 gauge shotguns. But there are more. While not as common, there are also 10 gauge, 16 gauge and 28 gauge shotguns. Of course, if you live in the UK, shotguns sizes are referred to "bore" and not gauge.

So here you are thinking, "no big deal, shotguns have gauges." And you might assume that the bigger the gauge, the bigger the shotgun. But you'd be wrong. Because it's backwards. Shotguns with smaller gauge numbers actually have larger diameter barrels. So a 12 gauge shotgun is bigger than a 28 gauge shotgun. Why you ask? Well, it's kind of interesting really.

Gauge in this context is a measure of weight. More specifically, it refers to the weight of a lead sphere, measured in fractions of a pound, that will fit into a given diameter barrel. So if a shotgun has a barrel diameter just big enough to fit a 1/12th of a pound lead sphere, then it's a 12 gauge. So a smaller diameter barrel, like a 28 gauge will fit a lighter weight lead sphere in the barrel, or in that case pellets that weigh 1/28th of a pound. Got it?

So now that gauges make complete sense, let's talk about a popular shotgun for beginners and experts - the 410. No worries, it's a 410 gauge right? Nope. It's a .410 caliber. This one is measured more like rifles and pistols where the name refers to the diameter of the barrel in fractions of an inch. 41/100ths of an inch in this case. By the way, it works out to be a 67 gauge shotgun; although no one ever calls it that.

Aren't you glad you asked?

The 12 gauge and .410 shells both have size 7 ½ shot. The .410 just holds a lot less of it!

Types of Shotguns

Like handguns and rifles, shotguns have different types of actions.

Break-Action shotguns most commonly refer to double barrel shotguns. Barrels may be mounted side by side or over and under each other. Of course, break-action shotguns are available in single and even three barrel configurations.

Pump-Action shotguns use a sliding mechanism, operated with the non-firing support hand, to load a new shell into the chamber and eject fired shells. Each shot requires operation of the slide. Hollywood loves pump-action shotguns as the heroes and villains look especially studly when racking their pump-action shotguns as they enter battle.

Semi-Automatic Action shotguns use the power of gas and/or inertia from a fired shell to eject a spent shell and load a new one into the chamber. It's a nifty idea to use some of the energy to operate the gun and all else being equal, a semi-automatic shotgun feels like it has less recoil as some of the energy is "soaked up" by the action.

You might also run across some far less common shotgun actions including bolt action and lever action.

Myth: You Don't Need to Aim a Shotgun!

Not many people know this, but shotguns were invented by actor Val Kilmer for use in the movie Tombstone. Kilmer needed a weapon capable of taking out a whole posse of Clantons and McLaurys - without much aiming. Hence the invention of a weapon capable of being fired from the hip, while giving the camera a sexy look.

A lot of people believe shotguns are great home defense guns, and easy to use, because you don't really have to aim. If you just point one in the general direction and fire, it will clean house so to speak. Right?

Well, in *The Terminator* movie franchise, that's how they work. In the real world, shotguns need a little more skill in order to be effective.

Just because a shotgun fires multiple projectiles, BB's, pellets, buckshot or whatever you want to call them, that doesn't mean that the shot spreads out like a giant cloud of locust intent on devouring a field of ripe Okinawan Purple Sweet Potatoes. It's important to remember that the shot leaves the barrel of your shotgun in a "cloud" exactly the diameter of your barrel. That's a pretty small cloud. To put it in absolute terms, the shot "cloud" leaving a 12 gauge shotgun measures just about ¾ of an inch in diameter.

While it's true that shot projectiles spread out more the farther they travel from the barrel, they typically stay in a pretty tight pattern at realistic distances. That's what that shotgun barrel does after all - keep the shot all together while it launches towards the target. If we're talking self defense, a realistic distance is some fraction of the interior of your house - like across a room or down the hall.

Let's take a quick look at a couple of range tests to see exactly how much the shot spreads out at realistic "inside your home" distances.

First, we'll try buckshot. Buckshot loads contain a small number of very large pellets. In the first example, we're using 00 (double ought) buckshot shells, which have 9 pellets that measure just about ⅓ inch in diameter. Typically, buckshot loads like this one will only create a "cloud" a few inches in diameter at short distances.

If you choose to use shotshells with a smaller pellet size, the cloud of short will typically spread out a little bit faster. Even still, at short distances, we're still talking a few inches.

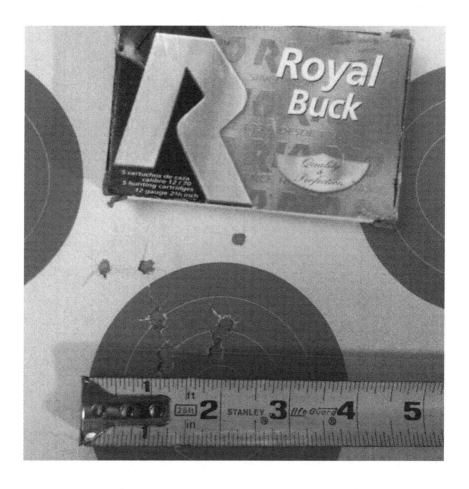

This 12 gauge buckshot (9 pellets) was fired at the target from a realistic "inside the house" distance of 18 feet.

Next, let's take a look at Number 1 size shot pellets. Number 1 size pellets are about .16" in diameter, or about half the size of the 00 buckshot we tested. The Remington shotshells we tested contain about 125 of the Number 1 pellets per shell.

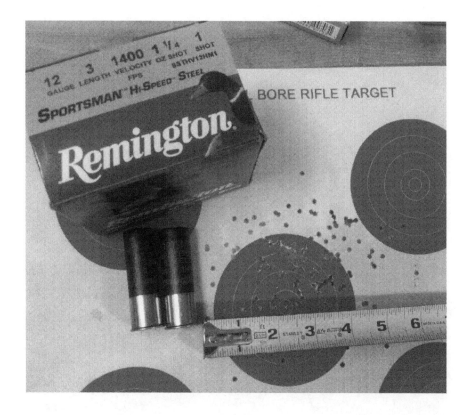

This number 1 shot stayed in a pattern of about 6 inches in diameter at a distance of 18 feet.

Finally, we tried really small birdshot - Number 7 ½. These shells have pellets that are only 0.095" in diameter and each shell has about 390 pellets. As you can see, this very small shot spreads out even more, but still, at a distance of 18 feet, the pattern still falls within 6 inches with most of the density within a 3 inch circle.

The number 7 shot spread out to about 6 inches, but the most dense area was still within a 3 inch circle.

The shotgun we used for these simple tests was a Mossberg JM Pro. It has a buttstock that's just about 12" long. So if you held it like a club and tried to whack someone with it, you'd have to aim less than if you fired it.

The bottom line?

You still have to aim a shotgun.

CHAPTER 4 - Things To Consider When Choosing Your First Gun

Try before you buy!

The very best way to buy your first gun is to hire an instructor for an hour or so and ask him or her to bring a few different guns. Any experienced instructor will have a variety of guns. If they don't, look for a new instructor! Have them show you some of the basic shooting skills with a couple of different guns. You'll quickly see what you like - and what you don't. As an added bonus, having a qualified instructor supervise you will ensure that you are handling each type of gun correctly so you can make a fair appraisal. Many a fine gun has been tossed aside when a new shooter didn't know how to handle it properly.

What defines the "right" gun for you?

The "right" gun is the most powerful one with which you can hit your target consistently. If that's a .22 caliber pistol, then so be it. A .22 pistol that hits your intended target is more effective than a .45 caliber that misses. Make no mistake, bigger and more powerful is always better for self-defense, right up to the point where you can still safely and properly handle the gun. But many new shooters need time, training and experience to reach their "full-power" potential. Start with what you can control and move up from there.

Bigger is actually better.

There is an assumed myth that large guns are too much to handle. First, let's define two types of "large." The first type is large size - as in length, height, width and weight. The second type of "large" refers to caliber or power. For the first type of "large" bigger is actually better. Here's why. Remember that guy Newton? Not Wayne Newton, the older, English one. He decided that every action has an equal and opposite reaction. So let's consider an extreme example. If you fire, say, a 9mm bullet from a 1 ounce pocket wonder gun, the same force as the 9mm bullet going 1,200 feet per second forward will be transmitted backward towards your wonder gun. Weighing only 1 ounce, it's probably going to fly at you like a drunk pterodactyl. Now, think about firing the same 9mm bullet from a 20 gajillion metric-ton pistol. The same force is being transmitted backwards, but you're not going to feel that gun move very much. All this goes to illustrate that while the recoil force of a given cartridge is the same, a larger gun will "soak it up" a bit more and the shot will feel less forceful to the shooter. Here's how it all nets out. A cute and portable 10 ounce pocket pistol will kick like an ill-tempered mule. The same cartridge fired from a full-size steel handgun will be quite comfortable to shoot. Make sense? So, don't choose a smaller caliber just because you tried a pocket cannon that weighs 4 ounces. Try a larger gun in the same caliber first. As you become more experienced, you can reduce the size and weight of the gun you carry with your chosen caliber.

Choose your own gun!

Ladies, we're generally speaking to you here. Husbands or boyfriends are NOT allowed to choose a gun for you! It's important for you to choose your own. The very best way to do this is to invest in item number one in this list - spending some quality time with a trainer. Preferably without your significant other there.

Try it on for size.

Just like a pair of boots or that cute little cocktail dress, you've got to try it on before you buy. It has to feel great in your hand. Even if you are not able to test shoot it, check to make sure that the grip fits your hand comfortably. Can you reach the trigger without stretching or changing your grip? Does your trigger finger rub along the side of the gun? If so, the grip is too large for you. Can you operate the controls easily with a normal grip? Can you rack the slide without weight training? If the answer is "no" don't rule out that gun just yet. See our tips on racking the slide like a pro later in the book. Using that technique, just about anyone can manage just about any modern pistol slide.

Carefully consider whether the price is right.

Most consumer product buying decisions don't have life and death consequences. Except of course Shake Weights. With guns, your life may very well depend on the quality of gun you buy. This is not a place to save a few bucks for the cheapest gun out there. The good news is that modern gun manufacturing techniques allow gun makers to produce fantastically reliable guns at very reasonable prices. If you stick with a big brand name, it's hard to go wrong these days. If your friend's cousin Cleetus bought a lathe and wants to make you a pistol, run, don't walk away.

Think about ammunition availability.

We've run across a lot of people who have bought some super-cheap surplus gun for self-defense. At deal time, buying a gun that was used in the battle of Stalingrad sounds charming and pocketbook-friendly. However, when it comes time to find self-defense ammunition, things aren't so rosy. Sure you can get 64 year old crates of surplus war ammo, but finding modern expanding ammunition that is safe and reliable is about as easy as getting Dianne Feinstein to speak at the NRA Annual Meeting.

CHAPTER 5 - How to Buy a Gun

Buying a gun is not all that complicated. Remember, it's a natural right, not a privilege. Our founders did not "grant" us the right to own a gun. They simply recognized that it is a fundamental human right and put language in place only to protect that right.

So when it comes to buying a gun, most of the process put in place by lawmakers to make things difficult is in direct contradiction to constitutional intent - and your rights.

Most people buy their guns from a local gun or big box sporting goods store, so we'll start there. However, buying a gun online is easy - and you just might benefit from a wider selection and lower prices. We'll talk about too. Finally, it's perfectly legal to buy a gun from friends, family and others with a couple of provisions.

What about gun shows? There's nothing mysterious there. Most people selling guns at gun shows are dealers, so the process is exactly like walking into a local store.

Gun shows are a great place to find unusual things - like surplus rifles wrapped in newspaper?

But first, let's address some strategies for surviving a visit to a gun store. It can be a bit intimidating if you've never been in one - but only because it's a new experience.

Let's see if we can remove some of the mystery...

Tips For A Successful Gun Store Visit

Not too long ago, a visit to a local gun store would more than likely involve meeting Clem, Bodean, and Clem's other brother Clem. They might be sitting around the store, with a few unemployed buddies, talking about yuppies who visit the store on occasion. The highlight of their day might have been glaring at "new people" who had not visited their store before.

Fortunately, those days are mostly behind us. Many gun stores have gone full-auto retail and implemented 20th century customer-centric ideas like hiring helpful sales staff, designing functional and attractive showrooms and running water. We love to see new stores competing with each other to offer even better customer experience. It's great for customers and the industry as a whole. The quality of buying experience is light years ahead of where it was just 10 years ago.

A good gun store, like East Coast Guns in Summerville, SC, will have a great selection of accessories like concealed carry gear, targets, sights, magazines and more.

Most cities now have more than one modern gun store, complete with shooting ranges and large showrooms for guns, accessories and ammunition. Stores like this are particularly helpful for new shooters as you can "rent" different guns at the stores' range to see which one you like - before you buy. And you can't beat the one-stop shopping convenience. You can buy a gun, a holster, safes and / or gun locks and cleaning supplies all in one place. Fantastic!

Even still, visiting your first gun store can be an intimidating experience. But so can any new experience where you have limited knowledge. Heck, I got a little stressed out going to Wild Birds Unlimited for the first time. I feared I would be instantly exposed as a bird-watching poseur!

We've put together a series of helpful tips to help you not only survive, but enjoy your first visit to a gun store.

Before you go

Think about your needs specific to a firearm. Do you want it for self-defense? Or just recreational shooting? Do you plan on hunting? Or maybe you want to get into competitive shooting. If the store you visit is on the ball, the first question they are going to ask you is what you want the gun for. This will help them steer you towards suitable options to meet that goal.

Think about bringing a friend who is knowledgeable about guns. Most gun owners truly enjoy helping others get involved in the shooting sports and they are always looking for an excuse to visit the gun store. "Honey, I can't work in the yard today, I have to help (your name) go find their first gun!"

"Never let someone else choose your gun and never buy the gun you plan to use for concealed carry without testing it. You won't know how it truly works for you until you shoot it, and if you lock yourself to a gun you end up hating, you won't have it when you need it."

~ Kimberly Walsh, Women's Self-Defense and Second Amendment Advocate, www.facebook.com/DamselProKimberlyWalsh

Figure out if the gun you want is really for you. Yes, this may sound a little weird, but unlike most any other product except maybe Cialis prescriptions, it's a federal felony to purchase a gun on someone else's behalf. This is one of those laws already in place to discourage convicted felons and those not legally allowed to possess guns from simply getting someone else to buy on their behalf. If the gun is going to be for you, great. If it's intended for someone else, bring them along so they can do the paperwork in their own name.

Think realistically about your budget. And I don't mean just the cost of the gun. If this is your first gun, be prepared to invest in accessories. You'll need a couple of very basic tools for cleaning. Do you have children in the house? If so, you'll need some way to lock up the gun. Even if you plan to just use your gun at a range, you'll need some type of hard or soft case to carry it in. You don't want to be walking around waving a loose gun! Fortunately most new guns come with a case. Gun locks are also easy to obtain. Most new guns come with one and most gun stores have simple gun locks available for no charge.

What to expect

Gun stores have to be careful. Like jewelry stores and other cash-heavy businesses you'll find that security is a little tighter than at your neighborhood Fabric World. You'll probably see cameras and possibly some sturdier than normal doors and windows. No worries, there's a lot of valuable stuff in the building and owners have to be careful. Most of what you'll see is for nighttime security. You don't often hear about gun stores getting robbed during business hours do you? Can't imagine why that is…

When you go inside, you might see that sales staff members are carrying guns! Yep. Just like the jeweler is most likely wearing some of his or her wares, employees of a gun store will likely be wearing some of theirs. Again, no worries! That's what they sell. It's also one of the reasons that you never hear about gun stores getting robbed.

Approaching and engaging the salesperson

OK, this is sort of a trick on my part. If someone doesn't acknowledge you when you enter the store, think about moving on to the next store. This has nothing to do with gun stores and everything to do with retail stores in general.

Like many jewelry stores, you might notice that gun store staff will only pull out one or two guns at a time. This is a simple security measure - just like those used for diamond rings. Unlike jewelry, gun store management is responsible to the federal government for each and every gun that passes through their store. If they lose one, they're not only out the cost of the gun, they are in serious hot water with the Feds. Given that the Bureau of Alcohol, Tobacco, Firearms and Explosives can revoke their license as easily as a Capitol Hill Lobbyist buys a round of drinks, owners have to be exceptionally careful.

When a salesperson hands you a gun to look at, you want to demonstrate safe and proper gun-handling procedures. Because it shows you know what you are doing. But more importantly because it's safe. Here are some things to consider:

Even though this is an "empty" gun, all of the safety rules outlined earlier in this book apply. Obey them religiously. There is no exception for the fact that you're in a gun store looking at an "unloaded" gun. Remember, a gun is ALWAYS loaded!

An on-the-ball salesperson will hand you the gun in a safe manner, perhaps with the grip first and the gun action open. If they don't, and hand you the gun with the muzzle pointed right at your body, you have a choice to make. If you're feeling dramatic, dive for the floor to get out of the line of fire. If you just want to subtly make a point, nudge the muzzle away from you while accepting the gun. Perhaps they'll get the hint. In all likelihood, you won't have to worry about this. In a really well run gun store, the salesperson will open and inspect the gun to make sure it's empty before even handing it to you. Then they will present it to you safely with the action open and the butt end first.

When you take the gun, return the safety favor and remember Rule 3. Make sure the muzzle never points at the salesperson or anyone else. The floor and ceiling are acceptable options depending on the store.

As soon as you get the gun, you want to open and inspect it. Look at the magazine and the chamber. Stick your finger in there to make sure it's empty. You may feel silly since the salesperson just did this, but you'll be safe. Remember, our goal is to enjoy this experience with minimal gunfire. Besides, if the person helping you knows what they're doing, they won't be offended that you're re-checking in the least.

They'll appreciate your attention to safety and good gun-handling practice.

Remember Rule 2 - Keep your finger off the trigger until ready to fire. When you're holding a gun to test it for size and feel, keep your trigger finger straight alongside the frame of the gun.

With most modern handguns, it's perfectly fine to pull the trigger to test it out. When I say perfectly fine, I mean that it won't harm the gun. If you want to test the trigger to see how it feels, first ask the salesperson if it's OK if you dry fire the gun. If they say yes, double check the "empty" status of the gun and point it at a safe backstop as you do so.

Dry Fire

Dry firing simply means going through the motions of shooting the gun, but with no ammunition. You're cocking the gun (if necessary) and pulling the trigger. This is typically done for practice or maybe to test out the action on a gun. By dry firing, you can get a really good feel for the quality of the trigger on a gun as there is none of that distracting flash and bang going on. There are serious safety procedures to consider when dry firing. Rather than repeat them here, we'll refer you to the section later in the book that discusses dry firing in detail.

Tell the sales staff your familiarity level with shooting right off the bat. If you don't know a firearm from fried okra, tell them. Be honest. The more the salesperson knows about your specific situation, the better they'll be able to help you. Pride and ego have no place here. You're investing in a piece of equipment that could save your life, so take full advantage of what the salesperson can teach you.

If the salesperson does not (immediately) ask what you want to use a gun for, either tell them, or move on to a different salesperson. There are tens of thousands of guns on the market, all with different design goals. You want to find the one that's right for your needs and if the salesperson doesn't know your needs, how will that work out?

Beyond your first store visit

Get multiple opinions. Like any other retail business, you'll encounter some sales folks who talk a convincing game, but don't really know as much as they should. Take your time, shop around and get opinions and advice from multiple stores. After a couple of visits, it will become clear who is steering you in the right direction.

Big box sporting stores like Cabelas, Bass Pro Shops, Academy Sports, Gander Mountain and others are spreading faster than hairballs at a Yeti convention. Like modern gun stores, these mega-stores are likely to carry everything you need. I've also found selection to be excellent and prices very competitive.

Which is better? That's your call entirely. It's hard to beat the value of a long-term relationship with a smaller business. You'll probably pay a bit more, but when you you need help down the road, the local business is likely to be there for you. If price is your primary consideration, then try some big box retailers.

One of the best things about buying from a local dealer is customization options. Check out this custom Duracoat finish by HHB Guns in Summerville, SC!

Buying Guns Online!

You can buy all sorts of things online.

The Jack LaLanne Power Juicer, Vince Shlomi's Slap-Chop food processor, the Ninja Cooking System and even a Brazilian Butt Lift kit. Not that I need a butt-lift kit.

You can even buy guns online. While not quite as easy as ordering the Proactiv Skin Care System, it's probably more fun.

How would you buy a gun online you ask? Well, let's start with a short quiz to check your internet armament shopping knowledge. After you answer, we'll take a closer look at why one answer is right and the others are incorrect.

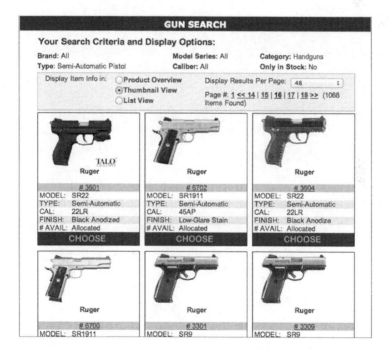

Buying guns online is easy. And the best part is near-infinite selection.

Pop Quiz!

Which of the following is an effective way to purchase a gun online?

A. *eBay.com - Search for "illegal assault weapons of doom" or something roughly equivalent. When you find a suitable match, bid like Congress investing in Solar Power companies until you win.*

B. *Craig's List - Check the listings in your area, hit the ATM for a wad of cash, and drive to your next encounter with destiny. Preferably alone and at night.*

C. *Answer one of those emails requesting your assistance moving $20 million into the United States. Perhaps the former Prime Minister of Mozambique wants to sell some guns before fleeing the country?*

D. *Visit a reputable online seller like GalleryOfGuns.com or GunUp.com.*

If you answered **A**, eBay.com, you made a valiant, common-sense effort, but unfortunately it won't work. You think Michael Bloomberg runs a nanny city? Try eBay. They run a nanny auction site. Every time the corporate coffee maker runs dry, eBay announces new restrictions about the things they won't sell. Like stuffed birds, military aircraft and ships, human body parts, or accessories for assault weapons. Just where are you supposed to find a spare gall bladder anyway? Just know that eBay frowns upon selling anything gun related. They know better than you what you want and need. Just accept it.

If you answered **B**, Craig's List, think for a minute. If a guy is selling a gun on Craig's List, and wants to meet you downtown at 2am because that's when he gets off work, you may want to reconsider you gun purchasing plan. You might be safer booking a trip to Ciudad Juárez, Mexico and telling a bartender you work for the Policia Federal. Ask him where you can buy a new service gun and some meth. I'm sure he'll be plenty helpful!

If you answered **C**, International Financier Connections, well, why not? The odds of legally getting a gun that way are just as solid as the odds of getting your 25% commission for your assistance with moving the former Prime Minister's fortune.

If you guessed **D**, you must be a gun guru. You're probably on the Department of Homeland Security's watch list because you're one of those pesky activists who understands things like laws. Watch your back!

That's right, it's perfectly legal to buy a gun online.

In fact, buying and selling guns is just about the most regulated activity there is. It's even more regulated than Jamie Lee Curtis after taping an entire season of Activia commercials.

Federal Firearms License or FFL

What's an FFL? That stands for Federal Firearms License. It's a piece of paper with words. It's also genuine, bona-fide proof from the US Government that says your firearms dealer is really a dealer. FFLs can also legally sell qualified individuals firearms in face-to-face transactions with the appropriate paperwork. In other words, FFLs are legally allowed to buy and sell guns for business purposes. Specific to buying guns online, when the selling dealer gets this FFL certificate from your dealer, they're able to exchange it for 500 prize tickets at Chuck E Cheese. Well, not really, but the FFL certificate gives the selling dealer proof and documentation that they can legally ship a firearm to another dealer.

OK, now that we're all clear on the specifics of the Gun Control Act of 1968 and FFLs, let's get back to the topic of how to buy a gun online. Perhaps the easiest way to explain the process is via a handy step by step guide.

How Online Gun Sales Work

The first concept to understand is that there is a thing called the Federal Government. They make laws and rules whenever they're not busy campaigning, having scandalous affairs and cheating on their taxes. One of the laws that the Federal Government has flatulated is the Gun Control Act of 1968. This law was established, in 1968, to codify many important things like common-sense limitations on the size of personal commemorative spoon collections. But for purposes of this topic, we'll limit our discussion to two components of the act:

1. Prohibition of direct sale or mail order of firearms across state lines.

2. Mandating the federal licensing of companies and individuals engaged in the business of selling firearms. Licensed organizations and individuals are commonly referred to as FFLs.

Steps to Buy a Gun Online!

1. **Google it!** Go to a reputable website and search for the gun you want. We're kind of partial to GalleryofGuns.com as they have a huge selection and pre-existing relationships with thousands of local dealers for delivery, but you can also find many reputable FFL dealers like GunUp.com that sell guns online. Be sure to get recommendations from folks in the know as to who is, and is not, reputable. If the web site you're buying from has a domain name that ends in .ru, .kp or .temporaryuntilinterpolfindsusagain you may want to keep looking.

2. **Buy it!** Once you find the gun you want, at the price you want, buy it! Most online sites will require full payment up front, but others like GalleryOfGuns.com operate through a collaborative effort with local dealers. In those cases, the online seller will take a deposit and you'll pay the balance when you pick up the gun. More on that in a minute.

3. **Don't get it!** Now that you have bought and paid for your gun, it will NOT be shipped to you!

4. **Send the paperwork!** The online seller will ask you to have a local (meaning in your state of residence) FFL dealer send them a copy of their FFL certificate. Your dealer's FFL certificate will have their local address so the selling dealer knows where to ship the gun.

5. **Wait!** At this point, the seller has your money, but they also have a document from your local dealer, certified by important government officials, that gives them an authorized shipping location.

6. **Wait!** The selling dealer writes down information about the sale in their books. These are called 'bound books' probably because they are bound to be audited by government officials at some point.

7. **Wait!** Next, the selling dealer ships your gun to your local (again, in-state) dealer. You still have not laid eyes on the gun you bought and paid for.

8. **Answer the phone!** When your dealer receives your gun, they write down more numbers and such in their bound book. Then they call you to come pick it up.

9. **Fill out paperwork!** When you go to pick up your gun, you will have to fill out a Form 4473. This is very similar to Form 4472, but one bigger. The Form 4473 requires you (the buyer) to fill out personal details like your name, birth date, citizenship information, favorite pastel color and whether or not you are hispanic. Yes, the most recent Form 4473 actually asks whether or not you're hispanic. We're not sure why. The Form 4473 also has lot's of true / false questions that inquire about your eligibility to buy a gun. Are you currently in jail? Have you been convicted of illegal things? Do you intend to buy this gun for yourself or to send to Syrian rebels? In short, you'll answer a dozen or so questions. Be truthful here as incorrectly filling out a Form 4473 is a big time crime.

10. **Listen in while your dealer talks to the Feds!** When you have filled out and signed the Form 4473, your FFL dealer will call the FBI. This part of the process is called a NICS check. NICS stands for National Instant Criminal Background Check System. Your dealer will read off some of the information you inked on the Form 4473 to the FBI person on the phone. Your FFL dealer will most likely sound bored and uninterested while speaking to the FBI as both parties do this about a thousand times a day. The FBI will check their records to make sure you are eligible to buy a gun. If you've been a good boy or girl, the background check will come back positive in a minute or so and the FBI will tell your FFL dealer to proceed with the sale. Not to cause alarm, but the process doesn't always work perfectly. So if you get a "no" response, don't panic. False rejections are not entirely unusual as people have similar names and, of course, you are dealing with the government! If you've behaved and still get rejected, your local dealer can help guide you for next steps to clear things up.

11. **Pay a few bucks!** Your FFL dealer will charge you some fee, usually $25 to $35 dollars for their trouble. After all, they need to send the seller their FFL, receive the shipment, process the paperwork, do a background check on you and store the records on the transaction forever. It's a big pain in the butt for your local dealer so don't complain too much about the transfer fee. Call your congress critter instead and ask them to repeal silly laws.

12. **Take your new gun home!** That's all there is to it! Now you get your gun!

Exceptions!

The above scenario applies to gun sales that go across state lines. If you see a gun advertised on the internet in your home state, you can certainly contact the seller and make arrangements to go see and buy the gun. The seller cannot ship the gun to you, but they can sell it to you directly. This is America after all and private sales between two individuals are perfectly legal. If the seller is an FFL dealer, you'll have to go to their location, fill out the same NICS background check paperwork and pass the check to get your gun. If the seller is a private individual not engaged in the business of buying and selling guns, you can meet that person to complete the transaction. Again, this scenario only applies when the seller and buyer are in the same state.

The Bottom Line

So, for all the political hoopla about getting guns online, background checks and the underground arms trade, buying and selling guns is a highly regulated process.

While it takes a few words to describe the process, it's actually pretty simple. Now that you know the specifics of the process, it might be helpful to relate a real online purchase I made recently as it's a lot easier than it sounds.

The Smith & Wesson M&P 15 VTAC was bought online from GunUp.com

Buying a Smith & Wesson M&P 15 VTAC - An online shopping experience

1. I shopped online at GunUp.com and found an awesome Smith & Wesson M&P 15 VTAC at a great price. I clicked the "buy" button and paid via a credit card.

2. I got an email from the sales team at GunUp.com asking for my FFL information.

3. I emailed my local FFL, HHB Guns, and asked them to send a copy of their FFL Certificate to the folks at GunUp.com.

4. About a week later, Henry at HHB guns called me and told me to come get my rifle.

5. I stopped by, filled out the Form 4473, listened to Henry's bored conversation with the FBI, and passed (whew!) my NICS check. It's a good thing I don't work for the Department of Justice or I might have been denied.

6. I paid Henry $20 (HHB Guns has a great deal on transfer fees!) and took my rifle home. I think Henry was kind of sad to see it leave as it's a really sweet rifle.

Piece of cake!

So here's the bottom line. I love shopping at local gun stores and shows. I often buy guns, accessories and supplies locally. But sometimes, that certain something you want is only available online. Or maybe you found a used gun on an auction site that you want to buy. Go ahead! While highly regulated, just like buying locally, purchasing online is safe, reliable and easy.

Family, Friends and Neighbors

Fine Print: I'm not a lawyer and I don't play one on TV. While the intent of this section is to provide some guidance on how you can legally buy and sell guns in today's political climate, the laws are changing as fast as former Governor Rod Blagojevich's trial testimony. Use this as a starting point, but be sure to check current laws and regulations in your country, state, county, city, neighborhood, block and living space.

We're going to keep this section short and sweet due to the rapidly changing legal landscape at time of this writing. With that said, much to Senator Dianne Feinstein's dismay, and at the time of this writing, it's perfectly legal to buy and sell a firearm in the United States. Do check again as the political maelstrom might have blown that right clean off the Constitution by the time you read this.

At time of this writing, it's perfectly legal to buy and sell guns privately - with a couple of provisions.

First, personal transactions require buyer and seller to be in the same state. If the transaction crosses state lines, even if the transfer is between family members, then you need to involve FFL dealers. Of course, the transaction also assumes that both parties are following state law.

Second, the buyer and seller need to have legal status to own a gun. So, for example, if one party is a convicted felon, the entire transaction is illegal.

The Bureau of Alcohol, Tobacco, Firearms and Explosives has national jurisdiction over these types of transactions and you can always check their website for current information.

http://www.atf.gov/content/firearms-frequently-asked-questions-unlicensed-persons#gca-unlicensed-transfer

"A person may sell a firearm to an unlicensed resident of his State, if he does not know or have reasonable cause to believe the person is prohibited from receiving or possessing firearms under Federal law. A person may loan or rent a firearm to a resident of any State for temporary use for lawful sporting purposes, if he does not know or have reasonable cause to believe the person is prohibited from receiving or

possessing firearms under Federal law. A person may sell or transfer a firearm to a licensee in any State. However, a firearm other than a curio or relic may not be transferred interstate to a licensed collector."

Bureau of Alcohol, Tobacco, Firearms and Explosives

At the end of this book, you'll find a "Cheat Sheets" chapter with handy links to gun law resources. Check those, and your local regulations to see what is and is not legal before you buy or sell guns privately.

CHAPTER 6 - Gun Holsters - Do It Right!

At this point, you've successfully navigated a gun store and come out alive. Hopefully you now own a few dozen new guns!

It's time to talk about one of the most important accessories you can buy - a quality holster.

Whether or not you plan to carry concealed, you really need a good, solid and safe holster. They're handy (and safe) to use at your range (specific range rules permitting.) You'll almost certainly need one to take any sort of self-defense class. And drawing a gun from a holster is one of those skills you should develop if you're going to own a gun.

Houston, we have a problem! Far too many new gun owners purchase a really nice gun, but then skimp on the quality of their holster. Seriously?

You wouldn't drink a Louis Roederer, 1990 Cristal Brut from a red Solo cup. Unless of course you're attending a Real Housewives of Yuleee, FL baby shower.

If you've been invited to carry the Dubai First Royale MasterCard, you certainly wouldn't whip it out at the Monte Carlo Van Cleef & Arpels from a velcro wallet. Unless you're total nouveau riche like Justin Bieber.

You wouldn't invest $15,000 in breast augmentation and buy Dollar Store Closeout brassieres. Unless, of course, you had just booked a gig on a new reality TV show.

So why do people think it's no big deal to buy a $9.95 holster from K-Mart for their brand new gun? It's not like it's a life and death investment. Or is it?

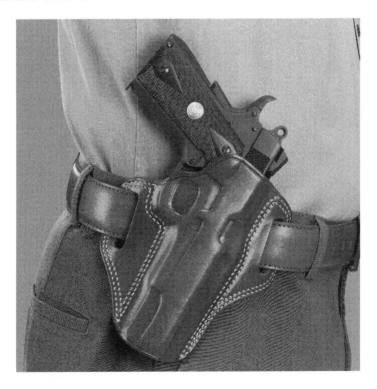

Here's one example of a quality holster. This one is a Galco Combat Master. Image: Galco Gunleather

Well, rather than address the wide world of gun holsters here, we're going to direct you to the Insanely Practical Guide to Gun Holsters. It's such an important topic, that we wrote a whole book on the subject.

You can find The Insanely Practical Guide to Gun Holsters at Amazon.com.

However, just to illustrate the importance of proper holster selection for your specific requirements, we'd like to share a personal story from the Insanely Practical Guide to Gun Holsters...

Let me tell you a holster tale. Unlike most fairy tales, this one ended kind of badly.

A Gun Holster Tale...

I started carrying a gun on a daily basis about 10 years ago. And when I decide to do something, I obsess... Big time. For example, after season 1 of The Walking Dead, when it became clear that zombies, along with personal injury attorneys, would one day rule the earth, I got serious about post-apocalypse survival tips. And I proceeded to learn to grow alfalfa in the bathtub, obtain drinking water with used Snuggies and milk the neighbors cat - which can be used to make a fine and aromatic Gruyère cheese by the way.

Back to holsters. When I got the shooting bug, I subscribed to every gun magazine known to man. American Handgunner. Guns Magazine. Guns and Ammo. Combat Handguns. Shooting Times. American Rifleman. American Cop. Concealed Carry Magazine. Redbook. Ok, so Redbook was for that great holiday cookie recipe, but all the others were for legitimate "gun learning" purposes. Anyway, I subscribed to hundreds, or maybe it was more like tens, of magazines per month. I bought books. And read them. Even ones with hardly any pictures.

In short, I thought I was learning everything I needed to know about concealed carry methods and proper holster selection. And so far, I had not been mugged, carjacked or teased about my sideburns, so I figured I had achieved concealed carry expertise. My strategy was sound and proven by several days of success on the street.

For a variety of reasons, I settled on a t-shirt carry method as my default. The brand is not important. Let's just say it was a spandexy model of shirt with holster pockets sewn into the shirt itself.

From my studies of many important books and magazines, I knew that torso carry on a t-shirt was not the ideal way to carry a gun. Access is significantly more difficult than from a belt-mounted holster. Although, on the plus side, you do get to give yourself a cheap feel during the draw. However, at that time of my life, absolute deep concealment was more important than immediate access. Or so I thought. And shirt holsters offer outstanding concealment. As an added benefit, those stretchy shirts can make you look far more buff than you actually are. In your own mind anyway.

To make a long story short, one day I was volunteering at a charity event and doing a fair bit of manual labor like setting up tents and chairs. As I quickly bent over to grab a tent peg, I had the disturbing sensation that all was not right in the world. But at that instant, I couldn't quite put my finger on specifically how The Force was out of harmony. At first, I thought my spider sense was telling me that Justin Bieber had suddenly hit puberty, forcing a sudden end to his singing and hair mousse modeling career. Fortunately that was not the case.

However, I did hear a small sonic boom resulting from my Glock 32 flying out of my shirt collar. I won't go into details, but lets just say the black Tenifer finish on a Glock creates an exothermic reaction when combined with sexy spandex, and the resulting forces are capable of launching a small object, like, oh, say a Glock, at a velocity of Pi times 10 to the 4th power. This is just shy of warp factor 3. Good work Scotty!

Being quick on my feet when it comes to avoiding major embarrassment, I immediately feigned a terrible case of irritable bunion syndrome and fell to the ground - conveniently covering up my now very exposed ground-dwelling pistol. Pointing towards the infirmary tent and yelling for bunion pads, I was able to draw attention away from myself long enough to re-holster my Glock in my suddenly untrustworthy shirt holster.

Did you catch that? Yes, it is in fact possible for a gun to launch out of an undershirt holster, through your regular shirt collar. At high speed. Complicated physics aside, the important thing is that it can actually happen. Prior to the event, this is not a scenario I would have dreamed possible.

Thanks to a genetic disposition to sudden bunion attacks and a little sleight of hand, I was able to avoid detection. This was somewhat of a miracle, as people tend to notice things like flying Glocks launching from beneath one's chin folds.

The morals of the story?

1. Do lots of homework before settling on your personal carry strategy.

2. Keep reading. Even books without pictures.

3. When you choose a holster, think about practical matters. Like bending over.

4. Always be prepared with a ready-to-go medical emergency in the event you need to create a quick diversion. I've already claimed spontaneous irritable bunion syndrome attacks, so you have to find your own.

But seriously folks, dedicate some time and funds to buying a proper holster for your gun. It's well worth it.

CHAPTER 7 - A Few Comments on Gun Handling

GUN TERMINOLOGY GONE BAD: NIGEL CONTINUES TO STRUGGLE WITH CONFUSING GUN EUPHEMISMS...

Far too often we hear about a serious accident involving someone and a gun. Statistically, gun-related accidents are quite rare, but even one is too many. Preventing a gun-related accident in your household requires a little knowledge and a lot of diligence.

In this section, we'll discuss some common best practices for gun handling. However, there are thousands of guns on the market, each with a slightly different mode of operation. Always refer to the manual for manufacturer recommended safety procedures. If you bought your gun used, no worries. Gun manufacturers are generally great about posting owners manuals online, so check their website for proper documentation for your specific gun.

We'll talk about some common gun handling procedures for different types of guns, but first, let's review some safety procedures common to most any gun.

The four cardinal rules of gun safety apply across the board. Treat all guns as if they are loaded. Keep your finger off the trigger until ready to fire. Never point a gun at anything you're not willing to destroy. Be sure of your target, and what's behind it. No exceptions.

For some reason, people just love to tinker with guns. Playing, fondling and maybe even caressing. Yes, a nice gun is a marvel of engineering and can be irresistible to touch. Unlike other items you might want to fondle, like maybe a kaleidoscope, there are serious consequences to careless gun handling. With guns, you really need to develop your own very rigid and inflexible processes for handling. Every single time you pick one up, you'll need to verify its loaded / unloaded status. You'll need to be sure that ammo is not nearby. A gun is just not something you want to pick up and put down at random. In general, avoid handling guns unless you have a specific reason to do so. Reasons might include use, cleaning, practice, or maintenance. Especially avoid handling loaded guns. If you carry a loaded gun, keep it in its holster when you take it off. The more you can do to minimize handling, the better.

When someone hands you a gun, whether it's in a store, at the range, in their house, or at an armory in Kandahar, Afghanistan, point it at something safe, like the floor, and immediately open the slide (or cylinder if it's a revolver) to verify that it is in fact unloaded. This is equally important for rifles and shotguns. Due to the wide variety of action types, we can't cover every type of procedure here. But we don't need to. Gun manufacturers do an excellent job of documenting safe procedures to loading, unloading and checking their specific models. Read that manual!

Do remember to keep your finger off the trigger while inspecting a gun. That alone will get you 12 extra bonus points! But still remember, a gun is ALWAYS loaded. Even after you've opened it to verify that it's empty. We know, it's kind of confusing. Just trust us on this one. If you pretend that it's always loaded, you'll never do something silly like pointing it at someone or something you really don't want to shoot.

When you pick up a semi-automatic pistol, always do two things right away. We're assuming you've already mastered Rule 1: Keep Your Finger off the Trigger Until Ready to Fire! First, while pointing the pistol in a safe direction, open the slide and check the magazine to make sure there are no cartridges loaded in the magazine. Second, and even more importantly, check the chamber to make sure there is not a cartridge in there. Now, even though you've verified that the gun is empty, treat it like it's loaded! Remember Rule 1?

Modern guns are designed with layers of safety features. One of the features that engineers include is prevention of discharge from unexpected impact. This is a fancy way of saying that most modern guns will NOT go off if you drop them and they hit the floor. In fact, you're far more likely to inadvertently press the trigger trying to catch a dropped gun. So, as hard and unnatural as it seems, if you lose control of your gun, let it fall. Any potential scratches or dings are far better than possible consequences of a negligent discharge.

The bottom line is that a carelessly handled gun can cause you to do life-altering and very permanent damage. Be careful out there folks!

CHAPTER 8 - A Fistful of Shooting Tips

We're going to talk about some basic shooting tips to get you started. But this book will never take the place of professional, in person, instruction. So run, don't walk, and find a shooting class in your area. Or invest in some 1:1 time with a qualified instructor. Nothing can take the place of a pro right there with you on the range. The store where you bought your gun should be able to help you get lined up with a good instructor. We've also included links in the Cheat Sheet section at the end of this book.

You can learn some amazing things from a good instructor. A couple of years ago, I took a one-day Defensive Handgun class from renowned instructors Tom and Lynn Givens of RangeMaster (www.rangemaster.com) and boy was that an enlightening experience! The most startling thing I learned was that Jesus was not going to load my gun. As Tom explained, when most people are in a fight for their very lives, and their gun runs dry, the tend to shout "Jesus!" As Tom further explained, Jesus might do other things, but he's probably not going to reload your gun, so you might as well do it! But seriously, we can't recommend quality training like that from RangeMaster enough. It just may save your life. Give Tom and Lynn a call, or check the back of this book for links to other training resources. You won't regret it.

So use this book as basic, starter knowledge. Don't let this book, or any other, take the place of personal instruction.

One more thing. We can't cover safe, operating instructions for every single pistol on the market in this book. So always read your owners manual carefully. It will show you exactly how to handle your gun safely.

"Ask questions. The gun world is a family and there is nothing we like more than welcoming new members."

~ Kimberly Walsh, Women's Self-Defense and Second Amendment Advocate, www.facebook.com/DamselProKimberlyWalsh

Stand Like You Mean Business

How to build a solid stance:

While the movie Weekend at Bernie's qualifies as a cult movie and spawned it's own cool dance moves, it really doesn't play well at the range. Mainly because dancing tends to throw off your aim.

Doing the Bernie simply refers to leaning backwards from the waist, so your shoulders are behind your belt line. Your head also leans back, like you're trying to stop a nose bleed.

This tendency to lean backwards away from the gun has no practical value. You see, there is little chance that your gun will suddenly turn around and start chasing you, so the position really provides no tactical advantage.

There are a couple of consequences to the Bernie lean that are pretty important. If you're already leaning backwards, you've given a big advantage to that recoil force that's about be applied to you. The bigger the gun, the more likely you are to be pushed off balance. Follow up shots are also more difficult as you have not provided a stable platform.

Speaking of stable platforms, semi-automatic pistols rely on the shooter pushing back against recoil force in order to operate correctly. The frame of a semi-automatic needs to be held stable in order for the slide and springs to do the work of ejecting a spent cartridge and loading a new one.

New shooters have a tendency to away from the loud flash and bag that's about to happen. Unfortunately, that's counter-productive!

You might hear about different styles of handgun stances like these:

The Weaver Stance: Place your support side foot forward of your shooting side foot. Put your shooting side arm straight out. Use your support hand to pull back on the gun, keeping your elbow bent, to create some isometric tension.

The Isosceles Stance: As the Sword of Damocles was made obsolete by guns, the Handgun Stance of Isosceles became cool. Keep both feet parallel to the target, shoulder width apart. Now shove both arms forward to form a triangle. That's where the "isosceles" part of Isosceles Stance comes from. Clever huh?

So which of these is right for you if you're going to ban the Bernie from your shooting? It doesn't make a darn bit of difference, because you can obtain a proper shooting stance with either of those methods–or some other.

Before worrying about the nuances of one technical stance over another, worry about getting your weight forward. It's pretty simple.

1. Place your feet about shoulder width apart.

2. If you like to put your weak side foot a little forward, great, do that.

3. If you prefer to keep your feet side by side, great, do that.

4. Flex your knees a bit. That makes the next step easier and gives you a better shock-absorbing platform. It also facilitates movement. Crazy things those knees!

5. Here's the important part. Bend a little forward at the waist. Your collarbone should be in front of your belt buckle. If you're not wearing a belt, pretend you are.

6. Roll your shoulders inward and down just a touch. That'll help control recoil even more.

7. Assume your Weaver, Isosceles, or Iron Lotus position. It doesn't matter.

8. Make sure those shoulders stay in front of your waist.

9. That's it!

You see, when it comes to killing Bernie (yet again) most of the battle is getting your body weight forward. The nuances of arms and feet positions are secondary to that.

You'll be amazed at how little your handgun recoils when you get your weight forward of your belt. You'll make that gun your bit... never mind. Let's just say you will be controlling your handgun–not the other way around.

After all, you never see Chuck Norris leaning away from those nameless henchmen do you?

Here's a proper handgun stance. Notice how the shoulders are in front of the belt buckle. She's controlling this gun, not the other way around.

Learn a Proper Grip

How to achieve a proper grip:

Friends don't let friends enjoy tea while shooting. Save it for the post range outing ice cream social.

If you watch some of the faux shooting shows on TV, you might hear someone mention a teacup grip. Some call it a cup and saucer grip. Just to be clear, this is not a compliment or indicator of social refinement. It's an observation of poor shooting form.

We're demonstrating TWO mistakes in this photo. Can you spot them both? Yep, hethe finger is on the trigger. And the dreaded cup and saucer grip technique.

If you're going to use two hands to shoot a handgun, you might as well get some benefit out of the support hand. Rather than cupping it under the base of the grip like a teacup saucer, how about snugging it right along side the grip so your support hand fingers can reach around the front? You'll be amazed at how little your feisty little pistol or revolver jumps when you use a proper grip. Lack of recoil control is a malady that affects millions of Americans. Only you can help by using a proper grip.

The cup and saucer grip simply refers to a handgun grip style where your support hand acts more like a tea set saucer than a support. The butt of your handgun simply rests on top of your open support hand palm.

Here's an example of a real coup and saucer grip. The support hand is not accomplishing anything productive.

Let's face it, if you're having tea with Prince Harry, you've got a tea cup in one hand and a saucer in the other. The cup holds the tea, so what purpose does the saucer underneath serve? Obviously it drives up the stock price for Royal Doulton China and adds complexity to the job description of footmen. Other than that, the saucer only serves to catch things that spill. It's a waste of a perfectly good hand that could be used to eat scones.

It's exactly the same with shooting. While your dominant shooting hand will be a little stronger, why waste all those nearly-as-strong muscles in the non-dominant hand? If you're simply resting your dominant hand and gun on top of a wimpy-looking hand-saucer, you're not getting any benefit from the support hand, are you?

So how do you achieve a proper handgun grip?

First, position the web of your hand as high as possible on the gun.

With your primary shooting hand, open your thumb and index finger. Push the web of your hand as high as it will comfortably go on the handgun grip, making sure that the barrel of the gun lines up with the bones in your forearm.

Note how the firing hand is high on the gun and the fingers are placed high against the bottom of the trigger guard. The trigger finger is placed alongside of the slide for safety.

Wrap your fingers around the front of the grip, making sure to keep your index finger out of the trigger.

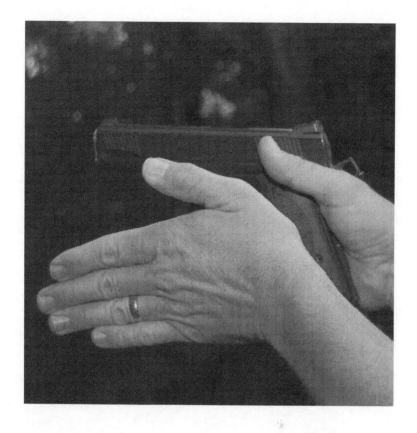

Your support hand palm goes right on the exposed area of the grip - again as high as possible.

Do you see some free space on the inside grip panel of your handgun? Good, that's where the bottom part of your support hand palm is going to go. Smack it on there and don't worry if there's not enough room to get your whole palm on the inside grip panel. There won't be and that's OK.

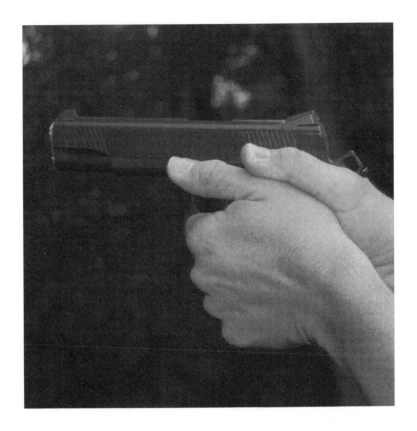

The final product. Support fingers are right up against the trigger guard and both thumbs are facing forward. We'll talk about that later.

Now wrap your support hand fingers around the front of your dominant hand fingers. Your support hand fingers should be high—to the point of pressing against the bottom of the trigger guard.

You'll know you've got it right if both of your thumbs are somewhere near parallel to each other and touching.

Next time you shoot, notice how much less your muzzle jumps. Your support hand can do wonders to help control recoil when you actually put it to work! Plus, a proper handgun grip looks really cool—you'll be a hit at the range. And those forward-facing thumbs? They naturally help you aim. Things tend to go where you point.

Use Natural Point of Aim

How to find your natural point of aim:

Water tends to run downhill.

Asparagus tends to find it way from kids' plates to the dog under the table.

And Michael Moore's muffin top tends to hang around his knees.

The point is, all things tend to gravitate towards their natural state.

If there was a way to let your body do more of the work of getting and staying on target, wouldn't you want to take advantage of that? Of course you would!

That's where natural point of aim comes in. When it comes to shooting rifles, handguns, or shotguns, natural point of aim simply means assuming the stance and position where your body naturally wants to point the gun. Perhaps the easiest way to illustrate natural point of aim is to look at unnatural point of aim.

Unnatural point of aim refers to any position where you have to "force" or "muscle" the sights of the gun onto the target. The most extreme example of unnatural point of aim would be standing with your back facing the intended target. If you could manage to get your gun pointed at the target from that position, it might be an example of supernatural point of aim. Less dramatic examples would be assuming any shooting position that requires you to move your arms, shoulders, waist, or hands to "force" the gun into alignment with the target.

If you have to expend any effort at all to "force" your gun to the target, you are creating fatigue in your muscles, eyes, and brain. The second you relax one or more of those, your gun will come off target.

It's one of those "oh, duh" things when you think about it. Shooting from a naturally relaxed and comfortable position will help you shoot more accurately, more consistently, and with better shot-to-shot performance. You'll also get the sights on target quicker if your body is already somewhat aligned when you look for that front sight.

How to find your natural point of aim

The best place to work on finding your natural point of aim is at the shooting range, mainly because it allows you to see your results as you practice. It's also safer because you're already in a place where you can point your gun safely at a target and backstop.

First, ensure your firearm is on safe and unloaded. Next, assume your normal shooting stance with your gun pointed at the intended target. Make sure your sights are lined up at a very specific point on the target.

Close your eyes. Take a couple of deep breaths. Think about all those who have passed before us. Do NOT try to force your gun to stay on target. Don't cheat. Remember what Miss Ninnymuggins used to say back in fifth grade: you're only hurting yourself! Just be natural for a sec—with your eyes closed.

Now open them. What do you see? Are your sights still lined up on the target?

If your sights are now lined up to one side or the other of your desired aiming point, that's an easy fix. Just have the range master move the target a bit to the side. But seriously, you can do a scaled-down version of the Ickey Shuffle to get your sights back on target. If you don't know what the Ickey Shuffle is, just Google "Best Football End Zone Dances Ever" and you'll get it. Simply put, shuffle your feet to realign your whole body so your sights line up on target.

If you find your sights pointed a bit high after opening your eyes, try moving your shooting hand side foot forward just a tad. That can

THE ROOKIE'S GUIDE TO GUNS & SHOOTING, HANDGUN EDITION

help lower your sights a bit. The opposite works if your aim point is low—move that same foot back just a touch.

Now, just to make sure you've really found your natural point of aim, briefly close your eyes again. When you open them are you still on target?

Repeat this exercise until your body position is just right.

Do this exercise repeatedly to make sure your stance is naturally consistent and aligned with your target. Soon, you won't have to close your eyes and dance anymore. You'll find that when you assume a shooting position, your body will find its natural point of aim.

Obviously this isn't something you will do in a tactical or self-defense shooting situation. "Hang on a sec! I need to find my natural point of aim!" The whole idea is to do this at the practice range in order to build a habit. After a few repetitions, you'll find that you naturally assume a stance that's correct relative to the target.

A Fistful of Shooting Tips   119

Become One with Your Front Sight

How to use your front sight:

Unless you have supernatural vision, you're going to notice a bit of a dilemma when you go to shoot your first target.

Your eyes can only truly focus on one thing, at one distance, at a one time. In handgun shooting, there are objects at three different distances that you need to worry about:

1. Rear sights

2. Front sight

3. Target

When you line up to shoot, there's a chance that all three of these may appear to be in focus to you. That's because the human brain is an awesome thing. It's processing all three and switching back and forth to create the appearance of simultaneous focus. Or something may look blurry. Different people see differently.

However, as a shooter, you'll need to learn to focus on just one of these objects, and that will be the front sight. It's OK if the target is a bit blurry - your brain figures it out and you can see it well enough.

Same with the rear sights. They are an aid to getting on target. It's the front sight that's most important.

This gets tricky when you're dealing with moving targets or high-stress situations. Your brain naturally wants to zero in on the target. But if you're not focused on the front sight, you'll miss.

So when you dry-fire practice (discussed later in the book) focus on that front sight. Like finding natural point of aim, it's a habit you want to build so you don't have to think about it.

You want to see something like this. The front sight is in focus and the rear sights and target are a bit blurry.

One more thought on that front sight. Like a golf or baseball swing, you want to follow through. Following through on your shot simply means keeping your eyes on the front sight until after the shot has left the gun. If your front sight stays on target before, during and after the shot, it's impossible to miss the target. So for each successful shot, you're really seeing two pictures - one before and another after.

Press, Don't Pull, the Trigger

Why not just pull it?

The number one cause of misses is a poor trigger press. By listening to shooters at the range, you might assume that a lot of guns shoot low. Or high. Or a bit to the left. Or especially a bit to the lower left.

In reality, it's almost always the shooter, not the gun, causing shots to go high, low, left or right. What's the last thing to happen before the bullet leaves the barrel? That's right, pressing the trigger.

Notice we say "press" and not "pull." Pulling the trigger implies a rougher and more aggressive motion. Like a Yeti stomping through the woods. You rarely see a Yeti glide through the woods right?

Here's the issue. Most handguns require from 3 ½ to 12 pounds of pressure to operate the trigger. Yet most handguns weigh from ½ to 3 pounds. So when you apply 5 ½ pounds of pressure to the trigger of a Glock 17 that weighs just over 2 pounds loaded, what tends to happen? Right, the gun wants to move!

So with handguns especially, since they don't weigh much, the shooter has to figure out how to apply those pounds of pressure to the trigger without moving the gun. At all.

That's where "press" comes into play. The fastest way to improve your shooting accuracy is to learn how to smoothly press the trigger without moving the gun. You also need to learn how to press your trigger finger independent of the rest of your hand. That's because the rest of your hand is holding the gun!

You'll hear shooters talk about "jerking" the trigger. If you look up "jerk" on Dictionary.com, you'll find a reference to a "spasmodic muscular movement." Spasmodic is generally not conducive to accurate shooting!

There's no magic secret other than focus and practice. While at the range, tune everything else out except making a smooth, motionless trigger press. Don't worry about accuracy yet. When you master a smooth trigger press, you'll soon see that all your shots tend to hit right near each other. You'll have a nice grouping of holes in the target. Once you reach that point, it's easy to place that group where you want.

Don't Be All Thumbs

How to keep your thumbs attached to your body:

The wrong thumb position may cause you to bleed all over the shooting range. We don't recommend it.

I can share this new-shooter tip from a vantage point of, ummm, let's call it personal experience.

Remember Ghostbusters? And how it's really bad to cross the streams of the Proton Pack particle accelerators? Well there's a similar rule of thumb (pun fully intended) for shooting semi-automatic pistols. Don't cross your thumbs as in the picture below. Sooner or later, that thing called a slide is going zoom backwards at Warp 17 and slice the dickens out of the webby, sensitive skin between your thumb and your index finger.

Slide

The slide is the portion of a semi-automatic pistol that sits on top of the gun frame and houses the barrel. When the gun fires, the slide moves backward very, very rapidly to eject the spent cartridge and load a new one. It's got really sharp edges on the bottom!

If you want to splatter copious amounts of blood around the range, feel free, but once is enough for me. Every single time I go to the range, I see new shooters crossing their thumbs while shooting a semi-automatic pistol. It's a mini-tragedy waiting to happen!

Trouble is on the horizon! If you cross your thumbs like this with a semi-automatic pistol, a bloodletting is inevitable!

Fortunately there's an easy way to avoid bleeding all over your range. Don't cross the streams. Point both thumbs forward and keep them on the weak hand side of your handgun. Your hand, and your local drug store, will thank you.

Revolvers present an exception. Since a revolver has no slide that zooms backwards, you don't have to worry about getting cut. In fact, many revolver shooters prefer to cross their thumbs. If you shoot a single-action revolver, that support hand thumb may be used to cock the hammer between shots.

Bottom line? Think about that grip. Because bleeding all over the range is embarrassing.

Rack the Slide Like a Pro

How to rack the most difficult slides:

Here's a stumper that derails many shooters. Racking the slide. With new guns and especially small, compact guns with strong springs, racking the slide can be a challenge. We constantly hear of new shooters turning down certain guns because they can't rack the slide.

Rack

To cycle the slide of a semi-automatic gun. Usually refers to the procedure of operating a handgun where complete cycling of the slide ejects an empty cartridge case (if present) from the chamber, while moving a new cartridge from the magazine into the chamber. This action basically clears the chamber of an existing empty, or full, cartridge and prepares the gun for firing a new cartridge. Repeated 'racking' of the slide will eventually empty the gun of all cartridges. Racking the slide is also used to clear jams or malfunctions. On the range, or in a competition, a command to rack the slide may be used in a couple of different circumstances. When a semi-automatic gun is first loaded, the slide must be racked to load a cartridge into the chamber so the gun is prepared to fire. Second, a range officer may issue a "rack the slide" command when shooting is finished to verify that your gun is empty.

Let us assure you, with very few exceptions, people are in fact stronger than the slide springs. Easily racking the slide on a semi-automatic handgun is a matter of technique.

The basic idea is to use natural leverage and strength points of your body. Without instruction, most folks will hold the gun with their firing hand and pinch the back of the slide with their support hand thumb and index finger to pull back the side. While the strong hand is perfectly capable of keeping the frame still against the spring pressure of the slide, those thumb and finger muscles are not exactly ideal for the job. You've got much larger arm and body muscles right nearby doing nothing, so why not use them?

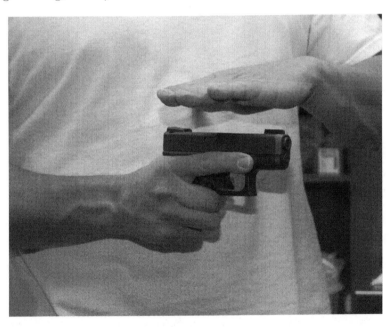

The key is to use big muscles to rack the slide. Here, I'm setting up the whole support hand to grasp the slide.

First, take a firing grip with your strong hand, making sure that your **FINGER IS OFF THE TRIGGER.**

Bring it close to your body as shown in the photo.

Next, flatten your support hand and turn it so your palm is facing the ground.

Extend your support hand thumb and jab it right into your sternum. Ouch!

Move your whole flat support hand over the back half of the slide of your gun.

Close it so that your palm is on one side of the slide and fingers on the other. Now you're grasping that slide with large hand and arm muscles instead of thumb and finger mini-muscles. Squeeze!

Keeping your support arm in the same place, push the bottom half (frame) of the gun forward like you're going to jab the target with the muzzle.

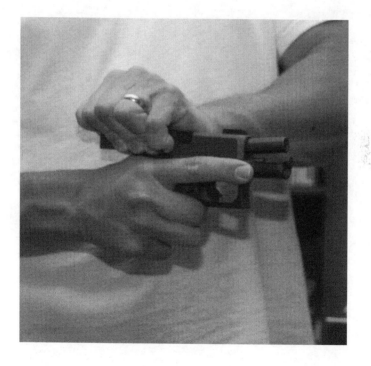

Notice how I'm using the firing hand to push the gun forward rather than trying to pull the slide back.

See what we did there? Rather than pulling the slide backwards, we're tricking you into pushing the whole gun forward.

When you have pushed the gun as far forward as the slide will allow it to go, quickly release the slide with your support hand. Let the springs snap the slide closed. Don't ever try to ease the slide back gently as the gun was designed to work properly when the springs do their job with gusto. If you try to be gentle and allow the slide to close slowly and gently, you're just asking for a malfunction.

How did that work out?

A word of caution! Be careful that you don't do the **side slide swipe**.

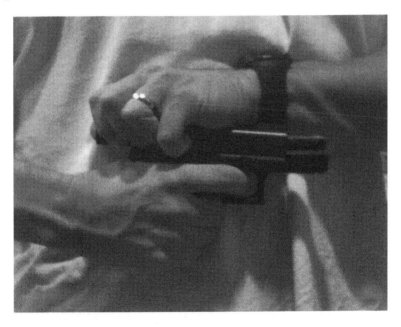

The side slide swipe! Not only is the gun pointed at someone to my left, there's a finger on the trigger!

We value our love handles. Don't shoot them off. Yes, dieting is hard, but far preferable to ballistic waist reduction.

The Side Slide Swipe happens when a shooter tries to rack the slide of a semi-automatic pistol. Given the simple geometry of us human folk, we generally have hands and arms mounted on the sides while the eyes face forward. So, standing at the range, naturally facing the target, the natural motion to rack a slide is (from a right handed point of view) **to point the gun to the left**, grasp the slide with your left hand, and rack. Nice and easy. The only real problem with this method is that your gun is pointed directly at all the shooters to the left of you.

It actually takes a bit of effort and concentration to rotate you body so that the gun is pointed downrange while racking the slide.

It's worth the trouble though. If not for yourself, do it for the love handles. Please.

Dry Fire and Practice at Home

How to safely dry fire:

When it comes to shooting, dry firing is a great thing that can dramatically improve your shooting skill.

Dry firing a gun simply means practicing the shooting motions without actually discharging a projectile.

We'll talk about the instructions on how to dry fire in a minute, but first I would like to make a money-back guarantee. If you properly (and safely) practice dry firing on a regular basis, your shooting skills will improve by 312%. Or maybe 31%. Or 19.3%. But they will improve. You can bank on that.

I like to think that dry fire practice and teeth flossing fall into the same general category. Neither activity is fun or sexy, but both make a huge difference over time. So if you want to have teeth like Tom Cruise or Julia Roberts, then commit to dry firing on a regular basis.

Let's talk about how to do it, without harming yourself, your family or your new love seat from Haverty's.

The most important consideration is safety. You have to develop your own method that insures that you will never, ever, ever have bullets anywhere near your gun when you dry fire. This is because you will be pulling the trigger on your actual firearm when not at the range. All of the safety rules we discussed earlier still apply. **You'll treat the gun like it's loaded. You'll keep your finger off the trigger until you're ready to fire. You won't point your gun at anything you're not willing to destroy - except perhaps that Haverty's love seat. And you'll be sure of your target, and**

what's behind it. We're going to follow all of these rules because if all the stars align just wrong, even for a second, and a live round is in your gun, you won't hurt anything except your pride and maybe an ottoman.

The first step is to remove all ammunition from your gun. Remove it all from your revolver's cylinder or the magazine in your semi-automatic. If you have a semi-automatic pistol, clear the round from the chamber. Stick your finger in there to make sure the chamber is empty. Now look at it. Now look through the magazine well and make sure you see nothing but air. Now do that again.

Those bullets you just removed from your gun? Take them into another room and set them somewhere you can see. Now count them. Are there as many there as were in your gun? Next take any full spare magazines you have and place those next to the bullets in the other room.

The end result of all this activity is that you have taken every round of live ammunition from your gun and anywhere else OUT of the room where you will be dry-firing.

While all this may sound excessive, just trust me and do it. Life has far too many distractions and interruptions to be anything less than obscenely safe. If all of your ammo is in a different room, preferably where you can see it from your dry fire practice area, there is simply not a chance that you will absent-mindedly fire a live cartridge.

My personal dry fire method!

I faithfully do all of the steps outlined above, but with a slight twist. You'll notice I recommended to place the live rounds in another room where you can see them. I do this to sp I can clearly see them near my dry fire target. I do this so that every time I pull the trigger on my gun while dry fire practicing, I am looking at the cartridges that were in my gun, but now in another room. When I dry fire practice in my office, I place the rounds on a dresser in the hallway. This dresser is visible from my office through a large doorway. So now, I'm using those live rounds near my target when I dry fire. If I am aiming at a dresser when I pull the trigger, and I see the rounds on top, they can't be in my gun, can they? Of course the dresser backs up to a stairwell and three walls. There is nothing behind it, so I also have a safe backstop. One other additional trick is to line up the cartridges from the magazine right next to each other. Then I take the cartridge from the chamber and place that an inch or so away from the others. So I have a visual cue of the 7 rounds that fit in the magazine of my gun, plus the round that was in the chamber. In a sense, I'm looking at a representation of the full capacity of my gun. The rounds in the magazine and the extra that was in the chamber.

Here's a dry-fire idea that works for me. I take the rounds out of the magazine and line them up near my dry fire target. I remove the round from the chamber and separate that from the others. If I am seeing these while dry-firing at my target, I know those rounds (plus the one in the chamber) are not in my gun!

How to practice with dry firing

Now that we've covered the safety aspects of dry fire practice, what do you do? Let's start simple and add practice exercises.

Basic dry firing simply allows you to practice pressing the trigger on your gun without all that distracting flash and bang. All kidding aside, it's a way to train your eyes, body and trigger finger to press the trigger smoothly, without moving the sights off target. The real benefit is that you can do all this without that instinctive flinch when the gun normally goes bang. By conditioning yourself to a smooth trigger press, without a flinch reaction, you'll eventually find that you do the same with a real gun when it does go bang.

After you've completed the safety procedures outlined above, just follow these steps according to what type of gun you have.

First a note about .22 handguns!

If you shoot a .22 pistol, you're better off NOT dry firing that gun. Most . 22's do not react well to dry firing due to how the firing pin is placed. Repeated dry firing of most .22 guns will cause damage to the firing mechanism. Most centerfire (see the "Ammunition Primer chapter) guns are perfectly safe to dry fire. Always check your owners manual to see what the manufacturer recommends.

Select your target. Get a comfortable stance. Find your natural point of aim by aiming at the target, then closing your eyes. When you open your eyes, are the sights still on target? If not, shift your stance and body position accordingly.

Here's a great place to pause and remember to focus on your front sight only. Remember, your eyes physically cannot have the rear sight, front sight and target all in sharp focus at the same time, so you have to pick one. Pick the front sight. The rear sight and the target should both be a little blurry. That's OK, you'll still hit the target.

Now, slowly PRESS the trigger as smoothly as possible. The goal is to complete the full trigger press until the gun's action releases - without moving the sights off target at all.

As the hammer (external, internal or striker) releases, see where the sights are aimed. That's where your shot would have hit had you been firing a live cartridge. Think of this last step as follow through. Train your eyes to see the sight alignment just after the gun "fires." Eventually, you'll know where your shot hit without looking at the target. You'll be "calling your shot." That's a really impressive gun term that simply says you know exactly where the shot impacted because, during your follow through, you were watching your sights relative to the target.

After your first shot, things will vary a bit depending on the type of gun you have, so let's take a quick look at the steps for each major handgun type.

Revolver (Double Action)

Revolvers are the easiest dry fire gun. After you complete the first dry fire "shot" you don't have to do anything to prepare the gun for the next shot. Simply get your body, grip and sight alignment back in place, aim at your target, and pull the trigger again.

Whether or not your revolver has a hammer, always practice it in double action mode. That is, pull the trigger without first cocking the hammer. That's how you would want to use the revolver in a defensive application anyway, so you might as well get used to it in practice. When you master dry firing a double action revolver without moving the sights off your target, you'll be a better shot than Ben Cartwright.

Semi-Automatic Pistols (Double / Single-Action)

With a double-action handgun you can configure your dry fire practice depending on what you want to accomplish. Like a double-action revolver, you can always just pull the trigger to simulate a full, double-action firing sequence. However, in real life, after that first double-action trigger pull, your handgun will cock itself so the second shot is a light trigger pull single-action motion. When you're dry firing, you'll have to pull back the hammer manually to prepare the gun for a single-action shot. So it's up to you if you want to simulate a first double-action shot, followed by a series of single-action shots or some other scenario. Do practice double-action shots, immediately followed by single-action shots though. The transition from heavier to lighter trigger takes some getting used to.

Single-Action Pistols and Revolvers

If you shoot a 1911 style handgun or a single-action revolver, dry fire practice is pretty straightforward. You're going to have to cock the hammer manually between each dry fire shot. With a single-action revolver, you want to make the hammer cock part of your dry fire sequence as you'll have to do that in real life. With a single-action pistol, you don't want to build a habit of cocking the hammer each time you pull the trigger. When you shoot live ammunition, the gun will cock itself after each shot so you don't have to. To help overcome building "bad muscle memory" when dry firing a single-action pistol, I like to fire the first shot, aim at a different target and simulate a trigger pull and repeat that a few times. After a few "shots" I bring the gun back from firing position, cock the hammer and repeat the exercise.

Striker-Fired Pistols

If you shoot a plastic fantastic pistol that's striker-fired, you have to cock the gun after each shot also. To do this with most striker-fired pistols, you have to rack the slide, as there is no hammer. Fortunately, you don't have to do a complete slide rack. With most pistols, you can pull the slide back ¼" or so and the striker mechanism will reset. Experiment with your gun to see how little of a partial slide rack you can get away with. Like the single-action pistol mentioned above, you don't want to build a habit of racking the slide after every shot, so vary your firing sequence accordingly.

These are different types of snap caps. Snap caps are inert cartridges used for dry fire practice. They allow you to practice magazine loading / unloading drills, and malfunction clearing and they save some wear and tear on the firing pin.

Add some complexity!

Hey, now that you've advanced beyond the simple certificate of participation for dry firing, you can add some steps to build your skills.

1. Draw from your holster! You've got an unloaded gun, in safe conditions. What better time to practice your draw? Practice drawing your gun, keeping your finger out of the trigger and evaluating potential targets. Mix in some more complex sequences where you draw your gun and dry fire one or more times. Be creative!

2. Practice magazine changes. How about dry firing your gun and pretending that was the last shot in your magazine? Practice dropping that magazine, pulling a new one and reloading your gun? Be extra careful that ALL magazines you use are empty!

3. Practice malfunction drills. When you dry fire, pretend your gun didn't go bang. What do you do? Practice the clearing drill depending on your particular gun. If it's a revolver, pull the trigger again. If it's a semi-automatic pistol, smack the bottom of the magazine to be sure it's seated, rack the slide, then re-evaluate the situation.

A dry firing tip...

Don't rush your dry firing. That's bad form and will help you develop rotten habits. Your brain is an amazing thing that will build memory of your actions regardless of the speed at which you complete them. Focus on completing your dry fire sequence slowly and perfectly each and every time. If you do that, speed will happen all on its own - perfectly.

Another dry firing tip...

After you're practiced a bit, balance a dime on top of your front sight. If you can complete a full trigger press without the dime falling off the front sight, you're getting good!

When you're ready to get serious...

Most people think of neutering in a bad way. My dogs run away for days when they hear that word. Recently we had to retrieve them from a snow cave just outside the town of Alert, located in Nunavut, Canada. In the case of the SIRT Training Pistol from Next Level Training, there really hasn't been a neutering of a pistol, technically speaking. More accurately, it's been designed as a eunuch.

The SIRT Training Pistol provides a great way to practice. By design, it's not capable of firing anything.

The SIRT is a practice-only pistol, made from the ground up as a practice-only pistol. It has a magazine, but you can't put cartridges in it. It has a slide, but the slide doesn't move. It has a trigger, but nothing fires - except a laser. Well two lasers actually. It has a magazine release button which drops the inert, but realistically weighted, magazine. It has a rail for tactical gun lights, rail mounted lasers, or even bayonets. If you want to make your eunuch dangerous.

In short, it has most of the components of a real pistol. But it's designed not to fire. Ever. And that's exactly what you're paying for. This 'firing challenged" capability makes the SIRT Training Pistol a great training aid. You can draw. As fast as you like. You can run around the house yelling things like "Freeze!" and you won't hurt anyone. You can aim at things (not people, people!) and pull the trigger. Thousands and thousands of times. And you will have zero risk of shooting the furniture.

The SIRT is modeled after a Glock 17/22. Same basic size, same basic weight, and same basic grip angle. The magazine is even the same size and approximately the same weight as a loaded Glock 17 magazine. Why a Glock? Well, at last count, 4,627% of law enforcement officers across the country use Glocks, so the potential LE training market for SIRT Training pistols is huge on this platform. Will Next Level Training offer other form factors? Perhaps, but I suppose that depends on market demand for specific models.

The slide on our tested SIRT is bright red. For most users of stock guns, this clearly differentiates the SIRT as a practice gun. If you're one to paint and personalize your real guns, simply do the same to your SIRT in a color that you recognize as "safe." So if your real gun really is red, make your SIRT blue. Or mauve. Or Hawaiian Sunset Lagoon Mango.

The SIRT features a standard front rail, so if you use a rail mounted light or laser on your real gun, you can put one on the SIRT also. Or you can mount a bayonet. And stab the sofa as you won't be accidentally shooting it.

One of the really big deals about the SIRT Training Pistol is the adjustable auto-resetting trigger. This means you can get as many trigger pulls as you want without doing anything to reset the trigger. It automatically resets just as a real trigger would when firing a real cartridge from a real gun. Want to practice double taps? Triple taps? Emptying the magazine to reload? No problem. As far as adjustment, depending on the model, you can tweak the initial trigger location, overtravel, take up force, and trigger break force. The trigger break can be adjusted from 2.5 to 12 pounds.

The SIRT comes in a durable hard plastic carrying case and includes an instructional DVD. We highly recommend it for practice!

Practice with a Purpose

How to become a better shooter by using less ammo:

Well, on second thought, there's nothing wrong with burning through ammo like Joe Biden burns through hair plugs. Just don't expect to become a better shooter as a result. Randomly adding hair plugs certainly hasn't helped Uncle Joe's hair. Like your shooting, he needs a strategic plan.

If you want to improve your skills, then you need to embrace boring things like goals and structure. But no worries, when it comes to shooting at the range, there are plenty of ways to have fun while improving your skills.

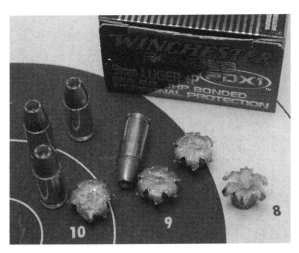

You can find a target with scoring rings like this one at any gun store or shooting range. Even Wal-Mart stores have them.

Measuring your progress doesn't have to be complex. You can do that as simply as using a standard round target with scoring rings. Pick a distance, like 5 yards for starters. Fire 10 shots at it. Add up your scores and write them down with the date. Next time you shoot, do the exact same thing. Pretty soon, you'll have a progression of scores from your outings to track progress.

When you have that down pat, you can graduate to paper plates!

The 45 Drill

Here's one that's simple and fun! It'll also help improve your practical shooting skill - getting shots on target accurately and quickly.

It's called the 45 drill because all you have to remember are four 5's.

- 5 inch target. We'll cheat a bit and just say paper plate. Because everyone has some laying around and they're small enough for this purpose.

- 5 yards. Position the targets five yards downrange.

- 5 shots. Clear enough?

- 5 seconds. Try to get all five shots to hit your paper plate target in five seconds or less.

That's a pretty straightforward drill right? The original intent of this drill is to accomplish the 5 shots in 5 seconds when drawing from a holster. But you can start on this one even before you learn how to safely use a holster. Just start from a low ready position. Get a proper grip on your gun and aim it at the ground five to ten feet in front of you. At the start of your five seconds, raise the gun, get on target and commence firing.

To accomplish the timing portion of the drill you can have a friend do it for you using "Start" and "Stop" commands. If you want to get fancy, and have a smartphone, there are free shot timer apps available. These have features that sound a starting beep, then listen for shots. The shot timer will show the number of seconds elapsed between the buzzer and last shot that it heard. You can also set "par time" which simply means you designate an interval, like five seconds, and the timer sounds a starting and ending beep.

The Dot Torture Drill

If I had to pick one practice routine, it would probably be the Dot Torture exercise.

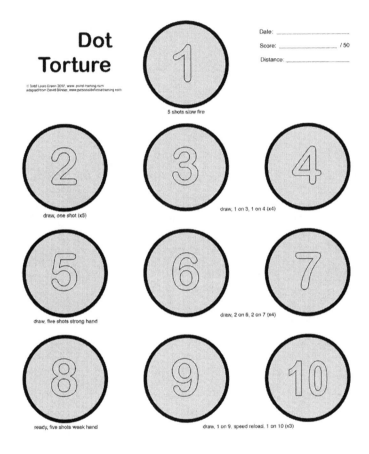

You can find Todd Louis Green's adaptation of the Dot Torture target at www.pistol-training.com.

As far as I can tell, this drill was designed by David Blinder at www.personaldefensetraining.com and modified by Todd Louis Green at www.pistol-training.com. What I like most about this drill is that it exercises a wide variety of handgun skills with one 50 round box of ammunition. The drill has you do slow and accurate fire, rapid single shots from a draw, multiple shots from a draw, single hand shots with each hand and even reloads. And the whole 50 round string of fire is scored so you can track your progress over time. Visit www.pistol-training.com to print the targets on standard notebook paper. Detailed instructions are on the target itself.

What if your gun jams?

How to deal with malfunctions:

The loudest sound in the known universe, other than Rosie O'Donnell, is the sound of a "click" when your gun is supposed to fire. We'll refer to that sounds as a malfunction. Sometimes there's not even a click and the gun still won't fire. We'll call that a malfunction too.

Fortunately, unless something physically broke on your gun between shots, malfunctions fall into a couple of common categories. We'll take a look at how to deal with them.

If you're at a retail or club shooting range, odds are pretty good that a Range Safety Officer is nearby. In that case, never hesitate to ask for help if you are not confident in what you're doing. Range Safety Officers deal with questions and malfunctions about a thousand times a day and will be able to help you out. Just put your gun down on the counter, muzzle facing down range, and seek help. Whatever you do, don't turn around with the gun in your hand and yell "Hey!" That will cause a ruckus for sure.

The Easiest One: Revolvers

If you shoot a revolver, you have the easiest job of all when it comes to dealing with a malfunction. If you hear a "click" just pull the trigger again. Odds are that you hit a dud cartridge that simply didn't ignite. While rare with quality factory ammunition, it does happen from time to time. If pulling the trigger a second time does not clear up the problem, then it's time to unload your revolver and seek additional help.

The Easier One: Failure to Feed / Failure to Eject

A semi-automatic pistol is a nifty invention. The "auto" part of semi-automatic refers to the fact that the gun is designed to automatically eject a spent cartridge casing and load a new one after each shot. Sometimes, things go wrong and the cartridge scheduled for forcible ejection doesn't want to leave. It's the same principle as those relatives from Ohahumpa, Florida who visit at Thanksgiving.

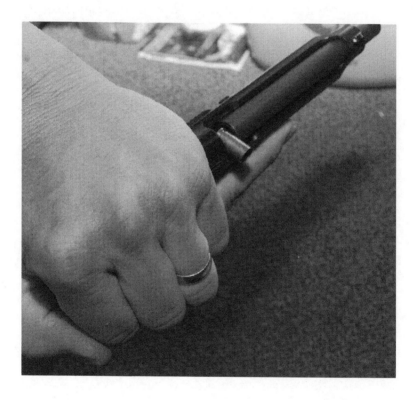

This malfunction is called a stovepipe. It's basically a failure to eject, which causes a failure to feed a new cartridge.

More often than not, a failure to eject is caused by the shooter. Semi-automatic pistols rely on the shooter holding the frame of the gun still during ejection so that the slide and springs have something to work against. If you use a weak grip, the gun moves backward with the slide and that whole bit of fancy recoil mechanism engineering fails. This may cause an empty cartridge case to get stuck in the ejection port. This blocks a new cartridge from being loaded and prevents the slide from closing fully. All this is a long way of saying the gun don't shoot no more.

Sometimes, the failure to eject or feed malfunction is caused by a magazine not being fully inserted into the gun. It may stay in place, but not be fully engaged. Guns aren't pansy toys, they're meant to be operated with vigor. So whenever you insert a new magazine into a semi-automatic pistol, smack it in there like you mean it.

Whatever the cause, to make the gun work again, you have to get rid of the spent cartridge casing and allow the slide to grab a fresh cartridge from the magazine and load it in the chamber.

Here's the solution: It's commonly called the Tap, Rack, Bang or sometimes Tap, Rack, Reassess drill. It works like this:

1. Keeping the gun pointed safely down range, enthusiastically smack the bottom of the magazine to make sure it's seated properly in place. Think of this as that first step to get your baby to breathe.

2. Rotate your pistol a bit to the right so the ejection port is facing towards the ground. Gravity helps here. Now rack the slide vigorously ONCE. This will (hopefully) clear any spent cartridge casings stuck in the ejection port and load a new round in the chamber. If you rack the slide more than once, you might be flinging perfectly good ammo from the magazine onto the floor.

3. Here's the "bang" part. But we prefer "reassess" - because you may not always want or need to shoot. Do things look normal again? Is the slide fully closed and in battery? "In battery" is one of those fancy gun terms that means "fully closed" by the way.

If this drill does not solve the problem, it's time to move to the next method of clearing, as you might very well have a double-feed malfunction

The Hard One: Double-Feed

The next most likely malfunction scenario is a beasty one. It's called a double-feed. And it's double-trouble because you have to do some rhythmic gymnastics to clear it.

The dreaded double-feed malfunction! This one requires you to lock the slide, tear out the magazine and rack the slide repeatedly before reloading.

1. The first step assumes you've already done the Tap, Rack, Bang/Reassess drill with no success.

2. Using the slide lock on your pistol, lock the slide to the rear, again keeping the muzzle pointed down range.

3. Remove the magazine. If you do have a double-feed, you're going to need to yank it out like an Esquire-reading yuppie from a Starbucks buffet. Things will be jammed up tight so use some muscle.

4. Save the magazine. You can tuck it under your shooting hand arm, stuff it in a pocket, or if you have the coordination of a mature spider monkey, hold it between a couple of fingers. You may need this magazine, especially if it's the only one you have!

5. Now rack the slide several times. There is no magazine in place so you don't have to worry about flinging perfectly good ammo all over the place. You're trying to clear out anything in the chamber area that might be jamming your gun.

6. Now replace the magazine and smack it into place.

7. Rack the slide one more time to chamber a round.

8. Unless your gun malfunctioned for some other reason, you should be good to go.

If these methods don't clear the problem, then there is more going on that we can't address in the scope of the book. Try getting help from the Range Officer!

Remember, if ever in doubt, ask for help!

CHAPTER 9 - Let's Go Shooting!

It's time to go to the range!

Like any new endeavor, the first visit can be fraught with uncertainty and doubt. But never fear, we're going to tell you exactly what to expect, so you can walk in with confidence and have some serious fun.

"Celebrate your successes and learn from your mistakes. Challenge yourself."

~ *Jennifer Oclaray Hast, Photographer, Shooter, Gun Blogger, www.injennifershead.com*

But first, let me share my first range experience. You can laugh at my expense and avoid those irrational fears I had…

A Gun Range Story

They say your life flashes before your eyes just before you die. I know this to be true because it happened to me.

About a hundred years ago, through a cosmic turn of events, I found myself at a shooting range for the very first time. Alone. I was clearly outnumbered by the one somewhat overweight and bored-looking guy behind the counter. And I was certainly out of my element - there was not a Starbucks anywhere in sight.

Suddenly, I understood what it felt like to be Attorney General Eric Holder heading out to testify on Capitol Hill – again. And I found myself completely empathizing with former Congressman Anthony Weiner – upon realization that you can't recall text messages. Doom. Armageddon. Sheer hopelessness. That impending feeling that all was lost.

I was mildly comforted with the knowledge that while I did not know a single thing about shooting, I was pretty sure which end of my gun to point forward. As I was about to fire the shot to be heard around the parking lot, time froze – and my life flashed before my eyes.

A gang of hoodlums busted through the door into the range. You could tell they had done this before, because they made it look easy, more like gently opening than busting and breaking, but I knew what they meant. I am not sure if they were Cripps, Bloods, or maybe some of the Latin Kings, but I was pretty sure they were up to no good. I couldn't see their tatoos, but they were probably just hidden under their Tommy Hilfiger sweaters.

They might have been a bunch of yahoos from an anti-government militia for all I knew. Actually, on closer examination, there was only one of them, but he seemed particularly ill-tempered. I knew he was looking for trouble and obviously intended to shoot me because... he had a gun. The fact that he was at a shooting range and wearing salmon colored slacks and a Lacoste polo shirt didn't fool me for one minute. Uh uh.

Needless to say, since I am writing this story, I somehow managed to survive. I think I managed to de-escalate the situation by nodding hello to the guy with a gun. Recognizing an equally tough thug, he nodded back.

At that point, I knew I had arrived. I was no longer a range virgin.

Be sure to check national and state parks near you. You might just luck out and find a beautiful - and free - range like this one!

What to Expect and Bring

Fortunately, checking into a shooting range is a lot less stressful than passing through a TSA checkpoint.

With that said, shooting range managers need to be careful as safety of patrons and staff is the number one concern. Many retail shooting ranges may want to take a quick look at what you are bringing into their facility. No, you won't have to go through any TSA porn scanners, but they may ask to look inside your shooting bag. Here's why.

Ammunition

Indoor shooting ranges have to worry about Rule 4 - be sure of your target and what's behind it - more than outdoor ranges. If projectiles exit the back of their building, the Jack In The Box down the street is going to be really upset. So if you visit an indoor shooting range, you might expect them to check your ammunition to make sure it's not of the steel-core, penetrator type. While great on enemy armor, these types of bullets wreak havoc on the backstops so many ranges prohibit their use.

The other thing many shooting ranges will check for is reloaded ammunition. While reloaded ammunition can be perfectly safe if you have loaded it yourself following all published safety guidelines, many ranges will not want liability. From their point of view, they don't know the source of reloaded ammunition and it makes little sense for them to take any risk of injury to nearby shooters in the event of a mishap. If your range does not allow reloaded ammunition, it's really not a conspiracy to increase profits - they are simply doing it for safety of all shooters present.

Eye and Ear Protection

Every range will have eye and ear protection available for sale or rent. But you really want to avoid that if you can. It's perfectly safe to use, but do you want someone else's ear sweat and eye juice on the stuff you rent? Nah. It's inexpensive and you'll want to have your own anyway. Let's talk about each for a minute.

OK confess. You don't particularly like to wear helmets while riding a bike either. It looks kind of dorky. And you're probably not going to fall on your head right? When it comes to the need for hearing protection at the shooting range, there is no probably. There is only absolutely. As in positively. Every shot you fire without ear protection WILL permanently damage your hearing. And each additional shot after that WILL damage it more. You probably won't know it for a while. Maybe years. But it WILL happen.

There are two basic types of ear protection. Inserts that you stuff into your ear canals like Genoa Salami and external ear muffs that make you look like a Top Gun pilot. Both can be effective if you buy quality. And getting quality ear protection is not all that expensive. You can find perfectly good hearing protection for $20 to $35 in most any gun store or big box sporting goods store.

Left to right: SureFire Sonic Defender inside-the-ear plugs, disposable foam plugs and Peltor external ear muffs.

Generally speaking, the exterior ear muffs will provide a little more protection, but some of the new internal models are getting pretty darn good. If you want to get really fancy, you can get interior or exterior ear protection that electronically monitors sound levels. Those let low level (safe sounds) like conversation get through to your ear, but block loud (and dangerous) noises like gunshots. You can find exterior earmuffs with electronic filtering for as little as $35. It's really nice to be able to hear your friends and the Range Safety Officer without removing your hearing protection.

Even electronic ear muffs, like these from Pro Ears, are relatively inexpensive. They allow you to hear range conversation while blocking dangerous noise levels.

Double Up!

If you're shooting at an indoor range, use BOTH interior and exterior hearing protection. Indoor shooting ranges are louder than a full-blown catfight on The View. So, to save your hearing, put some foam plugs in your ears, then add external muffs. You'll be glad you did!

Eye protection is equally, if not more, important. If you shoot, stuff may bounce back at you and hit you in the face. Bullet fragments. Target fragments. Backstop fragments. Irritable forest critters. And who knows what else? Unlikely, but is it worth the risk? While every shot without eye protection does not result in vision loss, it's only a matter of time before something wrecks one or both of your eyes. They don't react well to metal fragments and flaming powder gasses.

ESS Crossbow glasses offer excellent eye protection. This set has three inter-changeable lenses for different lighting conditions.

The easiest way to spot a new, and foolish, shooter is to look for those too cool to wear shooting glasses and ear protection. There are thousands of stylish eye and ear protection options out there so you can even look cool sporting your common sense safety gear.

Clothing

You wouldn't think you need to dress for the range. But you do. When you, or someone near you fires a shot, there is a miniature conflagration inside of the cartridge case. That makes recently fired cartridge cases very, very hot. Like really hot. Burning metal hot. So if you, or someone near you is shooting a semi-automatic pistol or rifle, it will be flinging burning hot brass all over the place. Here are a few apparel tips to help keep you on the rare, rather than well done side:

- Hat: A hat the covers the top of your head and that has a bill is a great idea. Even indoors. The brim will help prevent hot brass from falling on your face and worse yet, between your shooting glasses and your eyes.

- Covered shoes: Flip flops and sandals are not the best idea either. Think about how much it hurts when the top of your feet get sunburned. Now multiply that by 3 million degrees.

- Tight-necked shirt: Guys avoid loose and open buttondowns. Or button them up almost all the way. Ladies, watch the low-cut blouses - cleavage is not a good home for hot brass!

While avoiding getting burned by hot brass is a good idea, there's an even more important reason to dress properly. If you're shooting a loaded gun and hot brass starts to burn the bejeepers out of you, what's the natural reaction? Right. You're going to jump, move, dance, curse and many other things and who knows where that loaded gun will point in the process.

Gun Check

Some ranges may want to see the guns you intend to shoot. Again, this is a safety precaution. No range wants someone to attempt to shoot an unsafe gun, thereby endangering nearby shooters. Some indoor ranges are equipped to handle rifles up to a certain power level, so they may also want to check your rifle to make sure you won't blow out the back wall with your great-grandfathers elephant gun. Go with the flow. While these types of checks may seem annoying at first, soon you will appreciate the attention to safety. It's worth it.

Safety Briefing

Every shooting range has their own way of communicating range safety procedures and operations. Through the magic of VHS tape, some ranges are even automating this process. A couple of years ago, I visited Scottsdale Gun Club (www.scottsdalegunclub.com) - a huge indoor retail and shooting range facility. At that time, they required each first time range visitor to watch a 15 minute range procedures and safety video that outlined their rules and method of operation. The video even showed how to operate the automated target hangers. What a fantastic idea. As a shooter, I appreciated that everyone around me heard the exact same safety briefing. You may find that ranges have signs or verbal instructions to complete safety briefings. That's OK too, as long as they are thorough. If you end up at a shooting range that is not seemingly fanatical about safety procedures, turn around and find another one that is. It's your life after all.

If you have any questions at all about procedures, never hesitate to ask the range staff. They're there to help and are quite accustomed to helping new shooters get acclimated. Over the past year they have had more new shooters come to their business than ever before, so your questions are not new or unexpected. Experienced shooters love to help new shooters, so take full advantage of their goodwill.

Renting guns!

The first time I saw a "Guns for Rent!" sign at a Florida tourist destination, I thought the gun nuts had finally gone off the deep end. Of course, I assumed that one could just walk in, rent a gun, and carry it around town during their vacation. Ignorance is bliss...

Now that I know better, I can tell you that gun rentals are a great thing for new shooters. While you can't take them out of the store, you can try them out at the store's own gun range. Paying $10 or $20 to rent a gun is a lot better than dropping $600 on one that you find you don't really like. Most gun ranges have a wide selection of guns to rent. Take advantage of this, preferably before you buy. You can see what works for you before dropping the big bucks.

What to bring

You can buy pretty much anything you might need at a retail shooting range including ammunition, eye and ear protection and gun accessories. Over the years, I've found a few nice things to stuff into my shooting bag. This bag now weighs over 1,200 pounds and can hold a Volkswagen, but that's beside the point.

- Bandaids and cloth tape: Blisters happen. And you can't shoot just once. The more you shoot, the more likely you are to get a blister or two. Some Bandaids and tape for the fingers comes in handy.

- Extra eye and ear protection: You are planning on bringing friends right?

- Bug spray for outdoor ranges: Outdoor ranges tend to locate in rustic, woodsy places far from civilization - so you'll be sharing the range with mosquitoes, gnats and nomadic African bat bugs. Do yourself and your guests a favor and pack some Deep Woods OFF!

- Sunscreen for outdoor ranges: Back to that far from civilization and rustic thing. Some ranges have nice covered shooting areas and some do not. Plan on some serious sun if you're going to stay a couple of hours.

- A roll of tape: I like to keep a roll of regular masking tape in my shooting bag. It's handy for hanging or repairing targets or covering bullet holes so I can reuse targets.

- Stapler and extra staples: Depending on target stands at your range, staples might be more effective for hanging paper targets. Don't forget spare staples as the stapler always runs dry 19 seconds after you first use it.

- Extra targets for remote ranges: Indoor ranges will have plenty of targets of different types. Outdoor ranges may not. So keep some in your bag. There are thousands of fun targets that you can print on standard notebook paper available on the internet.

The last thing to expect is nice people! With rare exception, you won't find a nicer crowd of folks than at a shooting range. Don't be a bit surprised if the person next to you asks if you would like to try out their gun or strikes up a conversation about yours.

Shooting Range Etiquette

How do you make that first trip to the range, gun store, or even a friend's house to check out a gun or two without looking like a total doofus? Admit it, we all want to be cool and look comfortable and confident when learning new shooting tips and gun handling skills. Like all new things, learning how to handle guns can be intimidating. But how do you take the first step and learn basic gun and shooting rules and procedures now that Miss Manners' Sooper Dooper Guide to Shooting Etiquette is out of print?

Check out these range etiquette tips and you'll be safe AND looking like an pro shooter, or at least a well-rounded intermediate, in no time flat.

Case Your Guns!

Whether you're going to a public shooting range in the boonies or an indoor range downtown, you're going to have to get your guns from the car to the shooting bench. The very best way to do this is to have your guns in cases. Wandering through the parking lot and into the front door of a secure business waving a few guns around is a great way to have a really bad day. The safe and polite way is to bring your guns to the range in hard or soft cases. Preferably with the actions locked open so it's clear they are unloaded. Many ranges will want to take a look at your guns before you head to the shooting line, and if they see yours safely placed in a case, action open, they will be appreciative.

Don't Scratch the Itchy Trigger Finger

Yeah, I know, we keep harping on this trigger finger thing and the importance of keeping it off the trigger until you're ready to shoot. But we do that because folks violate this basic safety rule over and over and over again.

Apparently the best way to scratch your index finger while at the range is to rub it around the inside of the trigger guard. We know that index finger trouble is hard-wired into our human DNA, like nose picking at traffic lights, because we see it all the time.

Yes, the magnetic draw of a gun trigger is an irresistible force of nature for most index fingers – especially for new shooters. The millisecond that gun metal contacts the hand, the finger is magnetically latched on to the trigger. The finger just belongs there doesn't it? If it didn't why is there a big hole and a neat little handle to rest your finger on?

There's endless debate about the practical value, or lack thereof, of competitive shooting. One thing is for sure though. Enter a few IDPA or Steel Challenge matches and you will most certainly be cured of any trigger finger discipline problems.

Cold Range Means...

While not as frequent an event at indoor ranges, Cold Range scenarios are a regular part of shooting at many outdoor ranges and clubs. Basically calling Cold Range gives folks an opportunity to safely go downrange, change targets, clean up their mess, or whatever - without fear of getting shot in the backside. Cold Range means no shooting. While not as literal as "no shooting," a command of Cold Range also means "don't mess with your guns."

How can you be cold at the range? When you hear "Range Cold!" that means it's not hot. Which means there is no shooting. Or even pretending to shoot. Which means put your gun on the table. Which means don't play with it or show your friends anything about it that involves touching your gun. The table and the gun become one. A hot item. And you're suddenly the third wheel in that relationship. Keep it that way until you hear "Range Hot!" Then, and only then, you can try for a threesome with the gun / table love festival.

Yeah, we know. But your gun isn't loaded!

Do everyone a favor and save the hand trouble problems. Play a game of Angry Birds or catch up on some good old-fashioned texting while the range is cold. Just don't fondle your firearms.

Being cold at the shooting range isn't rude. Or event anti-social. In fact, it's not Cruel To Be Kind, it's cool to be kind. Kind of cold that is.

Bonus tip: If you want to look like a real pro, then don't just put your gun(s) on the table when you hear "Range Cold!" Step away from the shooting table and stay there the whole time the range is cold. This is a sooper dooper move that let's nearby shooters know that you are not messing with your gun(s) while the range is cold. It's very considerate and they will love you for it. Who knows? You might develop your own new relationship while your gun and the table are focused on theirs.

Many ranges allow shooters to reload magazines while the range is cold, as long as they are not messing with their guns.

When not actively shooting, it's a good practice to leave your gun locked open and facing down range.

Step Up To The Line

Back seat drivers are the worst. Frustrating, dangerous, and generally too wimpy to move forward and drive themselves. So are back seat shooters.

These are the ones that hang back too far behind the shooting line so that the muzzles of their various firearms are actually behind other shooters on either side of them. Is it the result of some instinctive Dirty Harry reflex to have the drop on everyone else at the range? We don't know, but as nice as you seem to be, I don't trust you! Not when you have a loaded gun behind my back anyway.

Step on up to the shooting line. Look at the bright side, you'll be a little closer to the target and shoot a better group!

This shooter is standing right up against the firing line. Notice how the gun is over the table, not a few feet behind.

No Hokey Pokey: Face Forward

Turning your self all around? No, that's not what it's all about at the range. Especially when you're holding a handgun.

Handguns are really short. Even shorter than Ryan Seacrest. That means when you turn your head around to say something like "Hey look! I just shot a pomegranite to smitherines!" your gun will most likely be pointing at the dude beside you or even someone behind you.

If you see people around you dropping like scandal-ridden Congressmen, it may be a result of your gun handling skills.

Feel free to put your handgun forward, and even put your right foot in. You can even do the Hokey Pokey, just don't turn yourself around.

Don't be shy about asking questions!

The best way to look like a pro shooter? Even if you're new to the whole thing? Ask questions! If you're not sure about something, just ask. You can even ask a pro. We've found them to be nice and helpful folks. It's OK. One of the most pleasant surprises from getting involved in the shooting community has been the overwhelming friendliness of the people. You just might be surprised how far people will go to help a new shooter.

Have fun, be safe, and ask a question if you're not sure!

CHAPTER 10 - An Ammunition Primer

Ha! An ammunition 'primer' Get it? If you don't, a primer is a component in a cartridge. So there's kind of a pun thing working there. Still not funny? Ok, let's move on...

Ballistics and ammunition performance is a complete field unto its own, which warrants volumes of research and observations. As this is an Insanely Practical Guide, we're going to hit on the high points. Things you need to know if you're going to own a gun. And since this is the Handgun Edition, we'll focus primarily on handgun ammunition, but venture into rifle and shotgun ammunition where warranted.

But first, let's clear something up. Hollywood does a lousy job of portraying the performance of handguns. Pistol shots cause villains to fly through windows, cars and buildings to explode and Piers Morgan to turn into a puddle of hysterical rubber cement. In other words, TV and movies show some serious knockdown power. Let's talk about knockdown power for just a sec...

Myth: Knockdown Power

Lot's of people educated on the internet talk about advanced gun topics like "Knockdown power."

As a completely unrelated side note, people that get their Masters Degree in ballistics from the internet keep people like me in business - making fun of them.

Remember that scene in the movie *Men in Black*? Where Tommy Lee Jones hands newly minted MIB Agent Will Smith a tiny silver alien pew-pew-pew pistol? Then when Smith fires it, he's knocked backwards 15 feet on his toucas? Well, that's how knockdown power would work in the real world. If your gun was capable of knocking someone down, you would be on the receiving end of some equally vicious recoil.

Here's why:

If someone tells you about the knockdown power of a given cartridge, immediately run to the nearest library and ask to borrow a copy of Physics For Dummies. In it, you might find mention of a guy named Isaac Newton.

While his brother Wayne was busy developing a fine singing career in Las Vegas, Isaac focused on important issues related to motion of objects. For example, if you buy the biggest gangsta pistol on the market, will it knock you over backwards when you fire it? Newton discovered that, no it won't, because for every action there is an equal and opposite reaction. So if you can hold and fire a gun without knocking yourself down, it's not very likely to knock down anyone you might shoot with it.

To test Newton's Fourth Law of Knockdown Power, simply take a bag of sand to the range and shoot it. Chances are it won't go flying through the backstop like the recipient of a Batman punch.

Rimfire and Centerfire

All modern ammunition works essentially the same way. Put it in a gun and it fires.

But seriously, it does all kind of work the same. Modern cartridges have the following components:

- **Primer**: Modern ammunition uses a magical chemical compound that basically explodes, or at least produces flames and sparks when it's impacted. The primer is struck by a firing pin in the gun, which then ignites the propellant charge in the cartridge.

- **Cartridge Case**: Usually constructed of brass, but sometimes steel, the cartridge case has either a hollow cup for a primer or a hollow base filled with primer compound. It also contains the propellant powder and holds the bullet or projectile in place.

- **Propellant Powder**: Back in the old days, cartridges used black powder which technically explodes. Modern cartridges use a variety of fast-burning (not explosive) propellants which create gas volume really, really fast. This expanding gas is what pushes the bullet down the barrel and out the muzzle.

- **Projectile or Bullet**: This is the thing that actually launches out of the gun. The rest either burns up or stays with the gun until ejected.

The only real difference between rimfire and centerfire ammunition is how the primer is placed and where the firing pin strikes.

Rimfire Ammunition

Rimfire ammunition has a hollow rim (hence the name rimfire) around the base of the cartridge. This hollow base is filled at the factory with priming compound. That's the magical stuff that explodes when you strike it with something. The firing pin strikes the outside edge of the cartridge, thereby completely squashing the priming compound underneath the firing pin. As the priming compound gets squished, it bursts into flame and ignites the propellant in the cartridge. This, in turn, makes a whole boatload of rapidly expanding gas, which propels the bullet forward.

Modern rimfire cartridges include the .22 Long Rifle, .22 Short, .22 Magnum, .17 Mach 2, .17 Hornady Magnum and .17 Winchester Super Magnum. Many others have come and gone, but you're likely to see these on store shelves. As the priming compound is "molded in" to the cartridge case, you can't reload rimfire ammunition as it's really hard to get priming compound in there.

Centerfire Ammunition

The primary difference between centerfire and rimfire ammunition is the location and method of primer insertion. Centerfire cartridges use a separate primer assembly which is about 4.287 times larger than the tip of a ballpoint pen. These separate primers are inserted into a hollow area at the base of the brass cartridge case. The hollow area just happens to be in the center, hence the name "centerfire." As the primer is a separate component, it can be removed after use and a new one inserted in its place. This allows folks to reload centerfire ammunition.

These two .223 Remington cartridge cases have centerfire primers, which are removable if you want to reload.

When it comes to rifle versus handgun, it makes no difference. There are centerfire rifles and handguns. There are also rimfire rifles and handguns. It's more of a cartridge thing.

Make sense?

Practice Ammunition

It's important to understand the difference between practice ammunition and self-defense ammunition. You can use self-defense ammunition for practice, although it will put a major dent in your wallet, but you really don't want to use practice ammunition for self-defense.

Practice ammunition is designed for... practice. At risk of offending my friends in the ammunition business, practice ammo is designed to:

- Fly forward when fired.

- Go as straight as possible.

- Go bang every time it's struck by a firing pin.

- Be relatively inexpensive in order to encourage people to practice more.

- Make holes in paper.

- Be safe to the shooter and the gun.

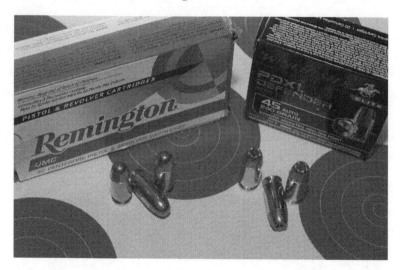

Practice ammo from Remington and self-defense ammo from Winchester. Both companies make excellent practice and self-defense ammo, these are just two examples.

Modern practice ammunition is excellent and exceeds all of these design parameters. It works. It's affordable. It's been proven safe and reliable by millions and millions of rounds fired by shooters like us, law enforcement and military personnel.

The only potential problem occurs when people ask it to do what it's not designed to do.

As we'll discuss in the next section, self-defense ammunition is designed to stop threats as quickly as possible. Not kill or wound, but stop. It's also designed to do that while minimizing the risk to others who may be behind the attacker. That's an important distinction. If someone is fighting for their life and fires a lethal round at the attacker that takes 10 minutes to kill that attacker, was it effective? Not really, as the immediate goal is to stop the attack as quickly as possible. A lot of damage can be done by a determined attacker in that 10 minutes. As a contrary example, what if that round never killed the attacker, but somehow discouraged them from continuing to attack? Effective? I would say yes.

Practice ammo is usually constructed in full metal jacket (FMJ) form. This simply means that the lead core of the projectile (bullet) is covered by a copper or similar metal to contain the lead and prevent it from gunking up the inside of gun barrels. When FMJ bullets hit something, they just keep going. They might get squashed a bit, or break apart in extreme cases, but generally they make relatively small holes in things and keep going.

When using this FMJ design in self-defense situations, this tendency to make small holes and keep going presents a problem. Making small holes in a determined attacker doesn't necessarily slow them down too much. Worse yet, FMJ bullets have a tendency to go right through relative soft targets and keep on going. So what, or whomever, is behind that attacker is now also in danger.

Strangely enough, studies have shown that FMJ ammunition is actually more lethal to the person being shot than expanding hollow-point ammunition as more shots are required to stop the attack. While not immediately lethal, the after effect of more shots increases lethality.

The net result is that you should always use practice ammunition for practice. Yes, it's dangerous and lethal to the attacker, but may be less effective as a defense tool and more dangerous to bystanders.

Self Defense Ammunition

Self-defense ammunition is expensive stuff, often approximately one dollar per round. That's because it is specifically engineered and manufactured to do amazing things.

Most defensive ammunition is designed to expand when it encounters a soft target like the human body. This expansion has two primary objectives.

First, it increases the size of the wound and likelihood of stopping an attacker.

Second, the expansion tends to dramatically slow down the projectile so it is less likely to exit the attacker and continue on to do harm elsewhere.

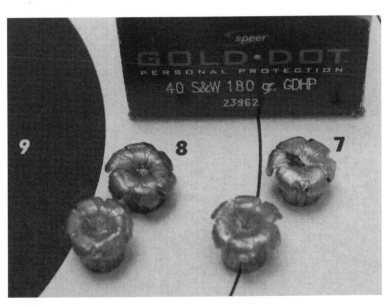

Speer Gold Dot is excellent self-defense ammunition. Note the consistent bullet expansion of these .40 Smith & Wesson projectiles.

In addition to these two characteristics, increased wound size and control of over-penetration, you have to consider **adequate penetration**. This is where the engineering magic comes into play.

The FBI and other law enforcement agencies have done extensive testing to determine just exactly how far a bullet needs to penetrate a target to be effective. Consideration needs to be given to barriers like clothing, jackets, bone, automobile windshields and other obstacles that may stand in the way of a projectile fired at a target.

Entire books are written on this topic alone, and we'll be publishing an Insanely Practical Guide to Handgun Ammunition in the future. For now, we'll keep it simple.

Some areas have prohibited traditional hollow-point ammunition. To address that problem, Federal has created expanding full-metal jacket ammunition that expands - just in a different way.

Your self-defense ammunition needs to provide adequate penetration, reliable expansion, and minimize over-penetration. Piece of cake right? Well, not really. That's why self-defense ammunition costs a dollar per round.

While most modern self-defense ammunition lives up to its marketing claims, there are still variables to consider. For example, the barrel length of your gun. You might have decided on a 9mm semi-automatic pistol as your handgun of choice. But 9mm semi-automatic pistols come in all shapes and sizes. Some have 2 inch barrels while others have 5 inch barrels. Barrel length is one of the variables that wreaks havoc on ammunition testing because the shorter the barrel, the lower the velocity of the bullet - all else being equal. In our testing, we've found (for handguns) that each single inch of barrel length reduction results in a velocity loss of about 30 feet per second. The velocity difference between the exact same self-defense cartridge in a 2 inch barrel gun and a 5 inch barrel gun can be 100 feet per second! As expansion performance of self-defense ammunition is correlated with velocity, that just might determine whether your bullet expands properly or not.

Since it's unlikely that you're going to test a bunch of bullets with fancy ballistic gelatin setups, stick with the big brand names like Speer, Federal, Winchester, Cor-Bon, Double-Tap and Buffalo Bore to name a few. We list a number of excellent ammunition manufacturers at the end of this book. Some manufacturers like Speer have developed special versions of ammunition for short-barreled guns. For example, they offer standard 9mm cartridges in their Gold Dot line, but they also offer Short Barrel 9mm Gold Dot cartridges. These are specifically engineered to properly expand at lower velocities while still providing adequate penetration.

Self-defense ammunition does not always expand. Be careful to choose the right match for your specific handgun.

One final note about self-defense ammunition. There are lots of advertisements for exotic self-defense ammunition that provides explosive performance of doom and destruction. You might hear claims that a single round can bring down a herd of irritable Wildebeests and that sort of thing. While much of this ammo has specific purpose, don't get sucked into the hype until you are confident and knowledgeable about exactly what you want your ammunition to do for you. Traditional hollow point ammunition is used by virtually every law enforcement officer in the country for a reason. It works and its performance has been documented for decades. If you ever find yourself in the situation of having to defend your choice of ammunition, wouldn't it be nice to say you simply chose the same ammunition that the local police force uses?

Reloading

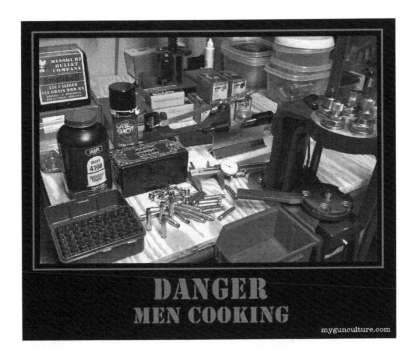

Reloading ammunition can be a great hobby for men, women and responsible young adults.

I'm one of those guys who enjoys reloading. Yes, I can save some money on a cost per round basis – if I place an hourly value on my time somewhere below the cost of 1/3 of a Wintergreen Tic Tac. The main reason I reload is that I like to tinker. Why experiment with 42 varieties of .357 Sig ammunition? Why shoot lead bullets at 1,000 feet per second out of my 1903 Springfield? Why not?

If you might have an interest in reloading in the future, start saving the brass cartridge casings now. If your range allows you to pick up your brass, you'll want to start saving your centerfire spent cartridges like 9mm, .38 Special, .40 Smith & Wesson, .45 ACP and other similar calibers. .22 Long Rifle is not reloadable as it uses priming compound built into the cartridge rim itself.

Cartridge components: primers, powder, cartridge cases and bullets.

While reloading is a science unto itself, we wanted to mention the idea here and point you to a couple of resources. Reloading manuals by powder and bullet manufacturers generally have introductory sections that describe the process of reloading in detail and provide reloading recipes.

If you can't wait for the Insanely Practical Guide to Reloading Ammunition, here are three excellent reloading books to get you started:

The ABC's of Reloading edited by C. Rodney James

Lyman 49th Edition Reloading Handbook

Speer Reloading Manual

CHAPTER 11 - Lights, Lasers and Accessories

Lights, lasers and night sights are not just cool, they dramatically improve your ability to safely use your gun in low light conditions. Not that you'll be shooting at the range in the dark, but if you choose to own a gun for self defense, statistics indicate that if you ever have to use it, it will most likely be at night.

Let's take a quick look at some things you can easily add to your gun to make it a more effective night-time tool.

Night Sights

Night sights ought to be required like seat belts, food labels and poop buckets for Clydesdales.

Well, required might be a little extreme, as many guns are purchased for daytime recreational use or other purposes. But if you own a self-defense gun that did not come with night sights, please seriously consider adding them.

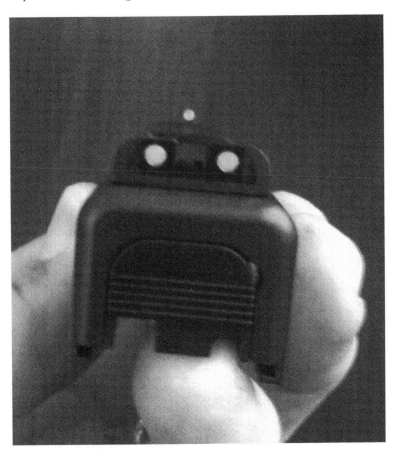

These TruGlo TFO Tritium Fiber Optic sights make a great upgrade that provides glow in the dark and improved daylight visibility.

In our opinion, the most effective night sights are ones that use tritium inserts. These are tiny crystal tubes filled with radioactive tritium gas, which apparently is something like Kryptonite. The important thing is that it glows at night and never requires a light source to initiate its glowing. So it's not like those star and moon stickers you plaster all over kids room ceilings. Normally, tritium sights will last about seven years before they start to go dim.

You can expect to pay between $100 and $130 for tritium sights for most pistols. There are all sorts on the market for most any modern handgun. We'll list a few of the major manufacturers here.

Trijicon www.trijicon.com

AmeriGlo www.ameriglo.net

XS Sight Systems www.xssights.com

Meprolight www.meprolight.com

TruGlo www.truglo.com

Depending on your specific gun, you may be able to swap the factory installed sights for night sights yourself, but many pistols really require a special sight pusher tool. The gun store that sells you the sights will almost certainly be able to install them for you.

Gun Lights

Having read millions of shooting articles, attended self-defense classes and shot hundreds of different guns over the past 15 years, I thought I knew the importance of weapon-mounted lights.

Then I shot Zombies in a cave.

Side view of the Crimson Trace Lightguard installed on a Springfield Armory 1911 TRP.

At the 2012 Shooting Industry Masters event, Surefire, a maker of tactical weapon-mounted and hand-held lights, set up a cave match. We're not talking virtual cave or simulated cave. We're talking the kind of cave you access by finding a hole in the middle of the woods. You then climb down a rotting ladder into the hole, squeeze your slightly-out-of-shape butt through a rocky entrance that's about three feet tall. You then crab crawl for a bit and navigate 20 yards or so of 18 inch wide winding crevasses. At this stage you can mostly walk. After proceeding another 100 feet or so into the cave you are completely blind. I mean completely. The match instructions were simple. Using a Glock equipped with a light and laser, you proceed deeper into the cave and shoot any 3 dimensional Zombie targets you can find. Without getting bitten. While Zombies aren't real, yet, and you're not likely to be clearing any caves with a Glock, the experience was very enlightening. Get it? Obviously, you had to see what you were shooting at, but this course also required some use of your support hand just to get around. Much like you might be fumbling around your house in the middle of the night.

Having the light on your gun frees up your other hand. In an ideal situation, you would use a hand-held light for navigation in the dark with your free hand. After all, you don't want to be pointing your gun at things until you know what they are. If they turn out to be a threat, that's when the weapon light comes into play.

The business end of a Crimson Trace Lightguard.

As you can see by these photos, weapon-mounted lights have gotten extremely small and light. The Crimson Trace Lightguard shown here weighs virtually nothing and adds no width or bulk to the gun. One thing to note is that you will need a holster that fits your gun with a light attached. No worries there, many holster makers are offering weapon-light ready designs.

A weapon-mounted light can make all the difference. This photo was taken in a completely dark garage. It's a Crimson Trace Railmaster light.

Laser Sights

Like weapon-mounted lights, laser sights are one of those things you don't fully appreciate until you try them.

Crimson Trace offers use-installable Lasergrip kits. In less than 5 minutes, this Glock 32 will have laser sighting.

Some instructors will scoff at laser sights because they insist that shooters should learn to use the iron sights on the gun. I couldn't agree more. All shooters should become proficient at shooting with iron sights. Those don't break or run out of battery juice, so you can count on them to work.

What laser sights do is add a new possibility to shooting options. Much like headlights on a car add the option of driving at night, laser sights add several new capabilities.

Here's the installed Crimson Trace Lasergrip on a Glock 32. When you grip the gun, the laser automatically activates.

First, they provide an excellent low-light sighting option. In dark conditions, the red (or green on more recent models) laser dot shows up brilliantly on your target.

Lasers make a great training aid, especially for dry-fire practice. If you are not executing a perfectly smooth trigger press, you'll see that laser dot bouncing around like Red-Bulled hamsters.

Lasers allow you to aim from unusual positions. If you shoot around a corner or obstacle, you might need to aim with the gun not exactly at eye level.

Lasers also support the natural tendency to focus on the target. Since the bullet strikes where the dot is, you can focus on the target and the dot simultaneously.

So, just as car headlights don't take away your daytime driving skills, lasers don't remove your ability to shoot with regular iron sights.

Wanna go first class? These Master Series Lasergrips fro Crimson Trace are made from real rosewood.

Crimson Trace (www.crimsontrace.com) offers a complete line of laser grips for nearly all modern handguns. What we like about the Crimson Trace offerings is that most models feature instinctive activation. The laser "switch" is either on the front, back or sides of the gun grip, so when you assume a normal firing grip, the laser is automatically activated. There is no need to remember to activate another switch or lever manually.

You might also want to take a look at offerings from LaserMax (www.lasermax.com) and Viridian (www.viridiangreenlaser.com.) Both make quality integrated laser products too.

Perhaps the best of all worlds for a home-defense gun is one with integrated light, laser and night sights. Yes, it will add a bit of bulk like the Glock in our photo. As you can see by the following picture, this setup provides options. You can use your iron sights or the laser dot right in the middle of the illuminated area.

This Glock with light and laser makes a pretty good bedside companion!

Here's a light and laser working together to illuminate and designate the target.

CHAPTER 12 - Care and Feeding of Your Gun

Cleaning Your Gun

If you want more than a simple certificate of participation as a shooter, then you need to think about how you're going to clean your guns. Modern guns are fantastically good at taking abuse from dirt and grime. However, there comes a time when you'll have to clean it.

Every gun has different safety procedures for field stripping.

Field Strip

No, field stripping has nothing to do with Woodstock flashbacks.

Field stripping simply refers to taking your gun partially apart in order to clean it.

Manufacturers design guns so that some of the major assemblies come apart fairly easily in order to make the gun easy to clean and lubricate.

After all, it's important that a gun be easy to disassemble and reassemble. If it's hard to put back together after a simple cleaning, then there's a chance it won't work right. And manufacturers certainly don't want to hear about someone's gun not working right when they really, really needed it. So a simple field stripping procedure is in everyone's best interest. Certainly yours!

We can't cover field stripping procedures here, so you'll have to refer to your owners manual. Be very careful about following instructions from the manual as many firearms require the trigger to be released as part of the field stripping procedure. Be triple sure that your gun is completely unloaded, chamber too, before starting to field strip!

A Beretta 92FS field stripped for cleaning.

Now go check your owners manual, carefully field strip your gun and come back. We'll wait...

First you're going to need some basic supplies. There are more gun cleaning supplies and magic solvents on the market than Barney Frank's nasal hairs, but don't let that discourage you. It's pretty hard to go too wrong with any gun-specific cleaners and oils. Notice we say gun-specific. What you don't want to do is use a general purpose penetrating oil like WD-40. We love WD-40 and it's wonderful for many things. You may even use it to clean gun parts. Just don't rely on it as a preservative and protectant for post-cleaning use. Guns tend to get really hot, hence the need for special oil and lubricant formulations that are designed to stand up to intense heat. Heck, you can even use motor oil to lubricate guns, so they're not all that picky.

At risk of setting a herd of apoplectic gun treatment vendors on my trail, I do want to highlight the importance of using the good stuff. Yes, motor oil will work. Save that for the apocalypse. As long as we have gun stores, use cleaners, lubricants and protectants that are specifically designed for guns. And they're not all the same. Some are designed specifically for cold conditions. Others are designed to operate dry so they don't attract fine sand into the guns' actions. Others are designed to clean only and not protect. Some are specifically designed to remove lead residue, others copper residue, others plastic residue from shotgun shells. The labels are very clear about this, so read carefully and experiment to your heart's content. You're not very likely to hurt anything. There is one caveat (or course!) and that is if your gun has part polymer construction, check to make sure your solvent is safe to use with polymer.

Once you've chosen your cleaner and lubricant - and sometimes they are in the same bottle - you'll need a couple of high tech tools and disposables to actually clean the gun.

Budget Gun Cleaning Mat

Get yourself a scrap of indoor-outdoor carpet for a cleaning pad. It's cheap as dirt, will not get all slimy with cleaning solutions and oil and does a great job of keeping small parts from rolling off the dining room table. You can find scraps for next to nothing at most home improvement stores. Your spouse will thank you.

One of my favorites is an old toothbrush. While rough on teeth, those nylon bristles aren't going to scratch gun metal or even the polymer frames on modern pistols. And they have a nice big handle so you can clean vigorously!

The next thing you'll need is something to clean out the inside of the bore (the barrel.) The traditional solution to this is a cleaning rod with a female threaded end. The end can accept an attachment that allows you to affix cloth patches for removing dirt, and cylindrical brushes for removing residue from the inside of the barrel. You can find these simple cleaning rods in kit form, complete with various size brushes and cloth patches at any gun store.

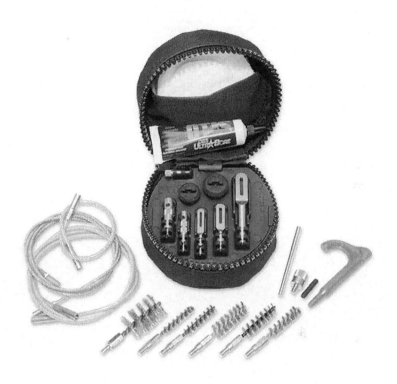

Here's the OTIS Tactical Cleaning System. The whole case is barely larger than a baseball. Image: OTIS Technology

We're going to pause and put in a plug for what I believe to be the best cleaning system on the market. It's called the OTIS Technology System. As the story goes, the founder of OTIS, Doreen Garrett, age 16 at the time, was hunting with her Dad and got hung up on a muddy root. Doreen and her Winchester rifle pitched headlong into mud, clogging up the barrel with swamp goop. In desperation, and trying to salvage the hunt, Doreen tried to use a stick to clear the mud and the stick promptly broke, clogging up the bore even more. With hunt-less hours in the cabin to reflect on solutions to the problem, Doreen dreamed up the OTIS System. From her experience, the system had to be field-portable. But also, it was designed to clean guns from the back to the front (breech to bore) to minimize risk of damaging the crown of the barrel. The result was design of a stiff, but flexible coated wire with various attachments for cleaning. As the "cleaning rod" was flexible, it could be rolled up into very portable field-ready kits. Now that's American ingenuity! So if you want to save yourself some trouble, consider getting an OTIS Technology System like the one shown here. It's well worth the money and the kits are designed to accommodate rifles, shotguns and pistols of various calibers.

Next, since your gun is field stripped, you have access to the barrel. Let's clean that first. Using the cleaning rod with a cleaning loop attached, stuff a cloth patch through the loop, apply some cleaner or solvent, and push (or pull) it through the barrel. Ideally do this from the breech to the muzzle as this will pull gunk away from the action and out the muzzle.

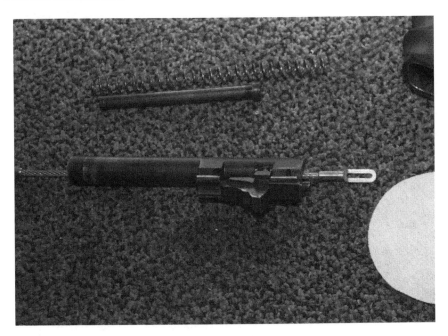

The brass cleaning loop attaches to the cleaning rod - in this case a flexible OTIS version - and holds the cleaning patch.

Once you have a cleaning patch attached to the loop, apply a little solvent to the cleaner and pull it through to remove loose dirt.

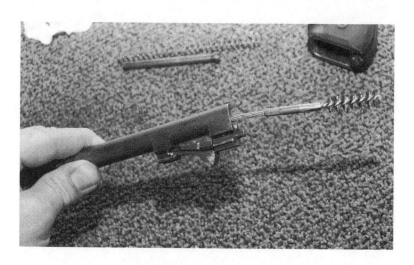

After the loose grime is removed with a wet patch, attach the caliber-specific brush to scrub the inside of the barrel.

Now you can attach a brass wire brush. Push or pull that through in the same direction a bunch of times. This will loosen stubborn stuff in the barrel like powder, lead and copper residue. The solvent you dragged through in the first step will be working to loosen dirt and mung while you do this. If you are cleaning a revolver, and want to do a bang up job, repeat these first two steps for the barrel and for each chamber in the cylinder.

Last, put your cleaning loop back on the rod and load it with a dry patch. Run that through. If it comes out dirty, put a clean patch on and repeat the process until no more dirt is coming out. Finally, check the instructions on the cleaner or lubricant you chose to see if they recommend leaving a light coat on the inside of the barrel. If you used a pure solvent or cleaner, you will need to finish the process with a fine film of lubricant or protectant.

Now you get to look for dirt on the rest of the gun. Be careful not to go crazy with that cleaning toothbrush as there are small parts and springs, like slide lock levers, that can get knocked off with vigorous cleaning. Until you learn the intricacies of your particular gun, be slow and methodical. Use a little cleaner, scrub with a brush, then wipe away dirt with a cloth cleaning patch or rag.

You probably want to clean your magazines as well. Wipe them down with a dry cloth and make sure you don't get oil inside the magazine. Oil and bullets don't mix all that well! Once in a while, you'll want to take apart your magazines and wipe the inside clean. They tend to accumulate dirt over time. Just refer to your manufacturer instructions.

The last step is to apply small amounts of lubricant. Your owners manual will show you the exact spots where this needs to be applied. Unless the manual says otherwise, less is more. The more oil you slather around, the more likely it is to attract dirt, so lubricate sparingly!

Modern guns are engineered to really take a beating and it's pretty unlikely that you'll do it any harm by cleaning. Relax, read your owners manual, and clean away!

Using all dry-fire precautions, test your gun to be sure you put things back together correctly. Some people like to clean their gun at the range when they are finished shooting. This way, after reassembly, they can fire a couple of test shots to make sure the gun is put back together in working order. That's another benefit of using one of the portable OTIS Technology kits.

Storing Your Gun

There are two major considerations to storing your guns.

First and foremost is safety. Anytime your gun is not on your person, you need to assume complete responsibility for its security. Is it safe from little hands? Is it out of sight from visitors? Is it in a safe condition - meaning locked away? Just be aware that some home, office and car solutions are intended to provide gun security and others are only intended to provide a simple holstering mechanism, so know the difference, and plan accordingly.

The second consideration is care. Are you storing your gun in such a way that it will not rust, accumulate grime or worse yet, dust bunnies?

Let's consider the first scenario - safety.

A cable lock like this one comes with most new guns. It goes through the action or cylinder to block the gun's operation.

Most guns sold in the US include a free safety lock. This is usually some sort of padlock but will vary depending on whether you have a rifle or pistol. Most pistols have a special type of padlock with a cable extension. The idea is to run the cable through the magazine well for semi-automatic pistols or the cylinder for revolvers, and lock it. The locked cable prevents the action or cylinder from closing, thereby rendering the gun safe and inoperable. You can't beat effectiveness of this system, but it can also be inconvenient if you want to use your gun for home defense.

One of the home storage products we cover in The Insanely Practical Guide to Gun Holsters is the GunVault.

The GunVault stores one or more guns safely in a steel mini-safe. Access via a touch keypad and/or fingerprint scanner is fast and easy - for the owner.

We've been using a GunVault MultiVault for years. The GunVault line is designed to provide security from children and guests. The sooper-dooper nifty part is that GunVaults provide security while still offering near instant accessibility to your gun.

We're huge fans of GunVault products and here's why.

They're designed from the ground up for you, and authorized users designated by you, only, to open easily in the dark. The original model featured a four finger button combination mechanism. The user sets a pattern of their choice. The buttons are recessed in four finger sized slots so the combination can be easily entered in the pitch dark. Newer models add the option of a fingerprint scanner. Simply swipe your finger and the vault opens. The BioMetric (fingerprint activated) model stores up to 15 fingerprints, so add fingers from both hands, from your spouse, and anyone else you want to have access. Either method is designed to be foolproof in the middle of the night with no visibility required — it's all done by touch.

The vault door is spring loaded. When the combination is entered, or fingerprint verified, the door springs open in a downward direction, allowing access to the vault contents.

The interior is foam lined. This not only protects your gun and accessories, but helps keep things quiet.

A number of options are available including an interior light, AC and/or battery power, and battery low indicators. The units all feature mounting holes and security cable attachment points so you can secure the whole vault to the floor, a wall or piece of furniture.

The MultiVault model is the larger version and features a removable interior shelf. You can store two handguns or keep a single handgun organized with other valuables, spare magazines or perhaps some secret plans for world domination. If you own one or more handguns, seriously consider getting a GunVault or something functionally equivalent to it.

Gun Storage Tips

Don't seal up your guns, let them breathe a bit. Gun cases are great for transport, but not so hot for longer term storage unless you plan to control humidity inside the case. If in doubt, think about how you would or would not store your smartphone for months or years at a time. I'm guessing you wouldn't leave it in the garage or that damp basement, right?

Fingerprints leave a little bit of salty residue on metal. The salt attracts water, which then develops rust. If you plant a nice, juicy fingerprint on a steel gun and leave it, you eventually see a rust colored fingerprint. If you handle your guns, be sure to wipe them down afterward with a rag with some gun oil. You can also find gun cloths already impregnated with silicone or some other metal preservative for the same purpose. If you want to go budget, just find an old cotton t-shirt and sprinkle some gun oil around it. Over time, the oil will spread throughout the shirt and it will become an excellent, and free, way to wipe down your guns.

If you're going to store your guns without use for a long time, you want to wipe them down with a preservative. There are literally dozens of preservatives on the market and just about any one will do for normal storage conditions. Check the retailers list at the end of this book to find a seller of preservatives.

Store your guns in conditions that you would also store Brown Sugar Cinnamon Pop Tarts. Not too hot, not too cold and relatively normal humidity. If Pop Tarts will last until their expiration date in your chosen storage area, then guns should be just fine too.

If your gun is going to be stored, make sure to remove all ammunition. Don't forget the cartridge in the chamber! Also, be sure to wipe off excess oil, gunk, or grease as they may gunkify even more over time.

If you keep your gun in a safe, be sure to include a drying agent or even a dehumidifier bar. Here are a couple of ideas to get you started:

Remington Mini-Dehumidifier, Rechargeable

Goldenrod Dehumidifier by Battenfield Technologies

Brownells Desi-Paks

CHAPTER 13 - The Second Amendment

Any time the subject of guns and shooting comes up, raw emotions are sure to surface. And those strong feelings are not just from hoplophobic and usually apoplectic people like Piers Morgan. Your friends, family and neighbors are likely to have very strong feelings one way or the other.

Why are gun rights such a big deal?

Why do we even have guns?

Why do folks get so darn upset when people start talking about gun control?

Why do politicians take positions that make less sense than Fabio joining the Hair Club for Men?

Perhaps a (mostly) true fairy tale about the Second Amendment will help explain why people get so doggone passionate about this stuff...

A Second Amendment Fairy Tale

Once upon a time…

In a faraway land called Murrica, there was a great struggle, lasting many days and nights. You see, the settlers of Murrica were tormented by an insatiable and covetous evil troll known as George Threepence. While George lived across the great waters, in the hinterlands, he insisted on taxing the settlers with many fees and regulations. After all, he did not get the name George Threepence for his generosity.

Fed up with overzealous overdraft fees and parking tickets without representation, the villagers of Murrica were desperate to be free of the troll. They called upon a new leader, George Chiseled-Face for help. George Chiseled-Face had a plan. He knew that the good people of Murrica were well schooled in the use of magic kablooey powder and many of them maintained stores of it for their personal protection and other uses.

Without delay, George Chiseled-Face rode throughout the land of Murrica, yelling at the top of his lungs, "Militia! Militia! That means you - all you settlers of Murrica!" And it was in this way, that the people of Murrica had determined to organize themselves into a fighting force to oust George Threepence, the troll. For the people did not trust big armies like George the troll had. They preferred to call themselves up to service and yell "Militia!" with great enthusiasm as needs arose. It was most exhilarating!

Using their wits, a collection of farm animals and copious quantities of magic kablooey powder, the good people of Murrica, led by George Chiseled-Face and many fair and white-wigged princes, fought battle after battle with troll George's Red Socks, until finally forcing them out at home plate.

Knowing the great responsibility that comes with independence, the settlers of Murrica began referring to themselves as citizens, believing that "serfs" and "settlers" were unbecoming descriptions for freedom-loving Murricans.

One of the first acts of the citizens of Murrica was to write things down on paper. These important ideas and observations were known as The Amendments. Even though the ideas written as The Amendments were thought to be so flipping obvious as not to need writing down, some of the older citizens knew better. Having fought trolls, gnomes and a few goblins in the past, the elder statesmen knew that some future idiot would try to change things because he thought he was really smart. Being very wise, all the citizens agreed on a bunch of Amendments over pizza, chicken wings and 14 gallons of hard cider.

The new citizens of Murrica knew the importance of being able to protect themselves against future trolls – whether said trolls came from across one of the great ponds, or from within. So they made it very clear that, forever and always, citizens of Murrica would maintain their stocks of magic kablooey powder.

This idea was so important to them that they wrote it down second, just after the idea about making sure they could always speak and write things down. This second idea, about keeping other people's grubby mitts off their magic kablooey powder, came to be known as the Second Amendment.

Many years went by and the citizens of Murrica suffered growing pains, a few wars and the invention of the Shake Weight. But all in all, the Murricans had developed a pretty good system of government.

During this time, most Murrican citizens never forgot the importance of The Amendments, especially the second one. They knew that George Chiseled-Face and his assemblage of white-wigged princes did exceptionally well on the SAT tests and had provided them with wise and timeless governing principles.

Over the years, the industrious Murricans developed many wonderful uses for magic kablooey powder. Like making beautiful light displays in the sky. They learned how to harvest wild animals to make bacon and roast beef using the magical kablooey powder. They even developed sporting contests using magic kablooey powder. While these other activities with magic kablooey powder were interesting and useful, the citizens never forgot the real reason that magic kablooey powder was protected by the Second Amendment. For it had enabled them to gain and maintain their freedom from the penurious and irritable troll, George.

Just to be sure, the citizens formed a new organization to help people remember the important lessons learned the hard way. The Nullifying Ridiculous and Rascally Administrative Actions Association (NRRAAA) was formed in 1871. Early activities were focused on helping teach people how to safely and effectively use magic kablooey powder. Later, the NRRAAA became more involved in politics of the land - often reminding princes and court jesters not to act like trolls. In one particularly famous miracle, at an annual assemblage of NRRAAA members, Moses of Heston made an appearance. He stunned those in attendance by freezing a rifle to his hands in order to prevent trolls from taking it while he slept.

From time to time, a bold gnome or troll would pretend to be a Murrican citizen and try to erase some of The Amendments. Fortunately Murricans were a pretty independent bunch, and TV had not been invented just yet, so they had numerous hours of free time. They paid attention to current events and stopped these trolls and gnomes right in their tracks. During those times, it sure was hard to fool a Murrican citizen.

Fortunately, the Nullifying Ridiculous and Rascally Administrative Actions Association (NRRAAA) attracted volunteers and leaders from all walks of life - ordinary citizens, princes and even minstrels.

Celebrities like Theodoric of Nooge joined the cause and soon, citizens of all ages were remembering The Amendments and learning how to safely and responsibly use magic kablooey powder.

Years had passed since the last insidious internal troll infiltration, and some citizens has forgotten the importance of The Amendments. And of course, by this time, none of them were alive when Murricans lived under the oppressive troll-thumb of George Threepence. During this time, shows like "I Dream of Jeanie" and "American Idol" were invented and this caused many Murrican citizens to succumb to a trance-like state of unawareness and apathy.

Just then, a charming new boy king was crowned in Murrica's capitol city of Deesee. While some Murricans were suspicious, many were entranced by his spell and ability to read poems from magical glass screen crystals. He filled his court with all manner of trolls, gnomes, goblins and even a few fairies. And all of them lived high on the pork in the glamorous capitol city of Deesee.

The new king also enjoyed the services of many court jesters who would do and say outrageous things in hopes of getting a few minutes of airtime on MSCNN, the boy king's personal scribe network.

Alas, the boy king encountered many difficulties as the land of Murrica was in turbulent times. Murrica had maxed out its Capitol One Murrica Card and rather than make minimum payments, the boy king decided to take out payday signature loans.

The bottom line was that the land faced a serious shortage of doubloons – and this caused great consternation. Citizens were lined up like never before at the boy king's court, demanding lower taxes, jobs and cell phones. Something had to be done! After all, the citizens of Murrica were not happy, and the king remembered that citizens in Murrica had magic kablooey powder. He was concerned that the citizens would revolt, as they did against George Threepence. The boy king decided to enlist the help of his court jesters to solve the problem.

The boy king's jesters studied the problem for many suns and moons. They even consulted the Oracle of Soros, but the Oracle of Soros was too busy straddling hedges to be of much help.

Suddenly, the boy king's prized magical talking donkey, Joseph, came up with an idea! "Perhaps we could disarm the angry citizens before they get entirely too upset! We could get our sorcerers to cast a spell on our subjects to make them believe that we're taking control of the magic kablooey powder for their own good and safety! But of course, we will have all the magic powder. This will allow us to do what we think is best for the citizens without interference."

The boy king was smart, and also a little bit sneaky, and thought Joseph the magical talking donkey had a wonderful plan.

The boy king proclaimed "Joseph! Gather all the other asses and implement this plan immediately! I will reward you greatly by allowing you to dine at my table with the minstrels from the western lands of Follywood Forest. They love to visit the royal palace and will entertain us and possibly stroke our egos. Perhaps the minstrels will assist you in your quest by making cheesy public service announcements!"

So Joseph went to work. First, he enlisted the help of some of his must trusted Rose Garden Gnomes. Sir Joe ManlyChin and Prince Patsy TooEasilyInfluenced were chosen to enlist the support of the majority of the Council of Inaction magistrates. Joseph knew that he could also rely on the magical powers of fossilized bones buried deep in the Council Chambers. Legends bespeak that the bones are the remains of an ancient hobgoblin, Harry the Misleader, believed to be a founding troll of the Council of Inaction. The legends also say Harry's bones would rattle occasionally during times of great political opportunity.

Joseph realized that not many people would listen to a magical talking ass, and knew that he needed to call upon the most enchanting sorcerers from the Teevee territories. He quickly dispatched his elves to locate them. After following a trail of New York Times clippings and Panera Bread crumbs, the elves found three of the most powerful sorcerers: WereWolf Blitzkrieg from the province of Concoction Narration Network, Boy Prince-in-Waiting Pierpont Morganstern and a sputtering goblin known as LudiChris Matt-P-U.

All had proven microphone-mojo magical powers of hysteria and would be most helpful with Joseph's quest. Joseph then asked the sorcerers to concoct enchantment fables, potions and mystical moving pictures that would entrance, entertain, and numb the citizens into a perpetual state of blissful unawareness. So they did.

The boy king had much power, in his own mind, but knew that he would need to enlist the full cooperation of the Council of Inaction. For if the Council of Inaction agreed to the plan, the citizens would certainly not doth protest too much.

The big day of the Council of Inaction vote arrived, and the king, his court and all the Rose Garden Gnomes, trolls, sorcerers and minstrels were most joyful, as the boy king's plans had never been thwarted.

But little did the king's court understand that a new gallant prince of the NRRAAA, Robin LaPierre and his band of Merry Riflemen, had been hard at work. Robin and his Merry Riflemen not only had knowledge of the magic kablooey powder, but even more importantly understood the powerful magic of the internet. For the internet had mystical power to shatter the sorcerers enchantment spells and deliver scrolls of truth to the citizens. While many citizens succumbed to the sorcerers moving picture spells, and continued watching reruns of The Bachelorette, a great multitude were able to see through the boy king's evil plot.

Late in the day, the Council withdrew to the secret chambers to consider the boy king's proclamation. Imagine the boy king's surprise when many of his magistrates on the Council of Inaction defied his instructions! He stormed and stomped and made vile threats of retribution. But the good citizens of Murrica were not afraid. For they knew that with the magic kablooey powder came freedom and independence.

To this very day, the boy king and his trolls, Rose Garden Gnomes and other insidious villains try to thwart the well-being of the citizens of Murrica. But they remain vigilant and sure, thanks to The Second Amendment.

Joining the NRA

If you're reading this book, you most likely own a gun, are thinking about buying a gun or at least have some interest in accumulating books.

If you fall into the first two groups, you need to consider joining the National Rifle Association. You see, when it comes to protecting gun rights, there is only one thing that really matters - the legislative process.

Under the legislative system, a body of lawmakers, comprised of recently-paroled Hair Club for Men customers meet every other Tuesday morning at Murray's Strip Club to discuss the nations problems and spray tanning. Occasionally, between rounds of Jello shots, the lawmakers will consider making changes to gun laws. Most of these decisions are influenced heavily by New York Mayor Michael Bloomberg, and of course Orange Sunshine LSD. So, left to their own devices, lawmakers will generally make decisions distinctly unfavorable to gun owners, the Second Amendment and the American way.

However, as we learned in the previous section, lawmakers in the Council of Inaction are most fearful of Robin LaPierre and his band of Merry Riflemen. Mainly because there are about 5 million members in Robins band. And periodically, these members vote to re-elect (or not) lawmakers to the Council of Inaction. So the lawmakers, being skilled at counting votes between acid trips, pay great attention to how many 'Murricans are part of the NRA.

So if you care about gun rights, the best way to protect them is to join the NRA and add to the number of members. Because the membership number is the only source of the NRA's clout with lawmakers. It has everything to do with the number before the six zeroes on the membership roster. If that number is 5, then the NRA can get some congress critters to consider their ideas if they ask real nice. If that number is 20,000,000, you'll see Harry Reid washing Wayne's car out in front of the Capitol. Or you just might see Harry Reid giving Wayne LaPierre a pedicure on the capitol steps while Dianne Feinstein details his Ford F350. And wouldn't that be nice?

People who play with guns have all sorts of reasons for not joining the NRA.

I forgot.

My dog ate my computer.

My dog peed on my computer.

I am a member – I sent them $10 twenty-seven years ago.

I bought a used gun, so I'm automatically a member.

Isn't it part of my AARP membership?

I have my voter registration card, so I'm a member.

I watch Top Shot on TV – doesn't that make me a member?

I got my membership in a box of Lucky Charms.

We've heard all the excuses. With that said, here's our Top 13 list of reasons NOT to join the NRA...

1. If more people join the NRA, then recently-deceased Hugo Chavez will have no chance of getting nominated to the United States Supreme Court. Be compassionate people! What's a dead dictator to do in his retirement years?

2. Operation Fast and Furious may be less fast and less furious with too much NRA oversight. If our government is going to export guns to Mexican drug lords, let's do it with style and plenty of volume – that's the American way!

3. I am married to: (fill in the blank) Eric Holder, Michael Bloomberg or Vladimir Putin.

4. If the NRA gets any more clout, those crazy Fast and Furious testimonies on CSPAN may come to a premature end. And everything else on daytime TV stinks now that All My Children is off the air.

5. Being part of the Vast Right Wing Conspiracy is so 1990's.

6. I've built my own intercontinental ballistic missile and the NRA is not fighting for my rights to cap it with a multiple-warhead nuclear bomb. It's my right!

7. I already get my gun rights news from The Huffington Post and New York Times. I've got my objective news sources covered already.

8. I don't want to encourage worldwide deforestation by adding my name to the NRA-ILA direct mail list.

9. Eddie the Eagle reminds me of clowns. And I have Coulrophobia . That's fear of clowns.

10. I already subscribe to Communist Dictators Quarterly magazine and don't really want another subscription to American Rifleman. I can only read so much propaganda in a months time.

11. What's a Constitution? Is that like when you eat too much cheese and get all backed up?

12. George Soros owns The Freedom Group, which owns all the gun companies, which own the NRA. But I don't subscribe to conspiracy theories.

13. They never serve Chateaubriand at Friends of NRA dinners.

But seriously folks. No excuses. If you own a gun, believe in little details like your right to life, liberty, and the pursuit of satellite TV, then you need to join the NRA.

Yeah, they've probably done something you disagree with, but so has your spouse/brother/sister/father/mother/child/neighbor. Are you married? If you have a disagreement about whether your spouse drank the last bit of apple juice, do you leave them forever? Because you don't like or agree with what they did? Well, think about getting married to the NRA. You won't always agree, but overall it's a good thing. With fringe benefits.

So get over it. Join all the other organizations you like. We do. There are a lot of great ones out there. Just be sure to add a +1 to that 5 million member number that freaks out all those certified politicians in Washington.

You can get more information on very inexpensive, and important, National Rifle Association Membership here:

National Rifle Association

http://home.nra.org/membership

Phone: 1-877-NRA-2000

CHAPTER 14 - Cheat Sheets

Where to Buy Online

In the "How to Buy a Gun" section of this book, we discussed the process to buy a gun online.

Of course there are other reasons to buy a gun online. Large online retailers may have much larger selections in addition to volume prices. Or, some online dealers specialize in rare or antique guns that may not be available locally. There are also auction sites which allow individuals to buy and sell guns through the site. Of course, all interstate transfers have to go through FFL dealers before delivery can take place.

Online Gun Retailers

Gallery Of Guns

www.galleryofguns.com

Davidson's Inc., the parent of Gallery of Guns is a gun wholesaler, selling to dealers nationwide. In 1998, Davidson's launched Gallery Of Guns to sell guns direct to consumers through local FFL dealer delivery. Gallery of Guns operates a large catalog website with tens of thousands of new guns from nearly every manufacturer. This is a fantastic way to buy factory new guns. Selection is huge, availability is great and prices are aggressive. From time of online purchase, you'll have your gun in a day or two unless your state has mandated waiting periods.

GunUp

www.gunup.com)

A newer player in the online gun sales market, GunUp.com does a stellar job of providing great service and great prices. Product availability is growing by the day, so sign up for their email alerts to get the latest on new arrivals. While specific terms may vary, at this time, GunUp.com is providing nice extras like additional magazines for certain firearms and a complimentary copy of GunUp Magazine. We've purchased a couple of guns from GunUp.com and highly recommend them.

Auction Sites

You may want to check out GunBroker.com and GunsAmerica.com if you're comfortable with auction sales. Sellers on both sites are a mix of dealers and private sellers. Of course, all firearms need to be shipped to a local dealer so you can complete your background check. Be very careful to study sellers' feedback ratings - we've had mixed results buying from auction sites. Just like eBay, some sellers with high volume can afford to get away with less than ideal service as they have thousands of transactions. You as the buyer only have one feedback, so your comments don't mean much if you have a bad experience.

Online Accessory and Parts Retailers

Brownells

www.brownells.com

Originally founded as a supplier to gunsmiths, Brownells has grown into a mega-one-stop-shop online retailer. They carry everything. And we mean everything. Accessories, parts, cleaning supplies, safety gear, ammunition, cases, magazines and more. If they don't have it, you probably don't really need it.

Midway USA

www.midwayusa.com

Like Brownells, MidwayUSA carries a huge selection of gear, parts, accessories, components, ammunition and more. We've dealt with them for years and years. You have to love how MidwayUSA supports the NRA and other shooting institutions. One last thing - be sure to check out the Clearance link on the home page from time to time. You never know what you'll find there and the deals are great.

Online Ammunition Retailers

It's easy to buy ammunition online. Most states allow you to purchase from online sources. But don't worry, these ammunition retailers will know the rules and whether they can legally ship to you. Even with shipping costs factored in, you might save a few bucks and benefit from big selections of available stock. If you don't see a retailer on this list, don't worry. These are just some of the ones where we've gotten great customer service over the years.

Brownells
www.brownells.com
Brownells entered the online ammunition business in the same manner they do everything else - with major attention to detail and customer service. We've never gone wrong buying anything from Brownells.

Lucky Gunner
www.luckygunner.com
LuckyGunner has invested in a fantastic online inventory system that only shows items that are in stock and ready for immediate shipment. If you see it on the website, it will ship immediately - usually on the same day. Prices are excellent and service is stellar.

GunBot
www.gunbot.net
A new and still-in-development tool, this website automatically searches the web for ammunition availability and prices. Very, very handy for quickly finding out who has ammo in stock. At time of this writing, similar search capability for reloading components is being developed.

MidSouth Shooters Supply
www.midsouthshooterssupply.com
Another longstanding general purpose retailer. You'll find ammunition, reloading supplies, shooting accessories and more at MidSouth.

Able's

www.ableammo.com

Yet another general shooting supply retailer, Able's carrys just about anything you need for hunting and general purpose shooting.

Georgia Arms

www.georgia-arms.com

I've used Georgia Arms ammo for years now and you can't beat the value. It's consistent and Georgia Arms offers bulk practice ammo in the form of "Canned Heat" and self-defense ammo that is an outstanding deal. Check them out. You'll also find that Georgia Arms runs booths at many local gun shows.

TJ Conevera

www.tjconevera.com

TJ Conevera focuses on reloading components and they do a stellar job of shipping products immediately. You also have to work pretty hard to find better prices. We can't recommend them highly enough.

Training, Dealers and Shooting Ranges

Online Training Resources

GunTalk TV
www.guntalk.tv

Tom and Ryan Gresham operate GunTalk.tv and a weekly radio show that focuses on, you guessed it, guns. Check out the TV site for dozens of free instructional videos. For a few dollars a month, you can get access to the whole library.

NSSF Videos
www.youtube.com/theNSSF

The National Shooting Sports Foundation operates a YouTube channel filled with tutorial videos. You can also subscribe to the NSSF Podcast for videos.

Brownells
www.brownells.com

You've got to check out the Brownells video library. They constantly produce quality videos with tips on gun cleaning, accessorizing and maintenance. Great stuff!

Training Programs

National Shooting Sports Foundation First Shots Program
www.nssf.org/FirstShots/Seminars

Learn to shoot at a First Shots seminar near you!

National Rifles Association Safety Programs
www.nrainstructors.org/searchcourse.aspx

Find a National Rifle Association safety class near you.

Thunder Ranch
www.thunderranchinc.com
Ready for some first-rate training combined with real hospitality?
Book early. Really early!

GunSite Academy
www.gunsite.com/main
One of the most established shooting schools, you can't go wrong
here.

RangeMaster
www.rangemaster.com
If you live in the eastern half of the US, check out RangeMaster.
Tom and Lynn Givens and staff provide outstanding self-defense
training.

Dealers

National Shooting Sports Foundation Dealers Directory
www.nssf.org/retailers/find/
Find a local gun dealer near you with NSSF's up to date listings.

Shooting Ranges

WhereToShoot.org
www.WhereToShoot.org
Find shooting ranges near you.

Competitive Shooting

One of the best ways to become a better shooter is to get involved with some local competitions. They are generally low-key, low-stress and high-fun. Never done one? No worries, just show up for a match. There will almost certainly be a new shooter orientation and if not, experienced shooters will be more than happy to help you.

Competitive shooting won't teach you combat or self-defense strategies, but it's a great way to learn how to operate your gun under a little bit of stress. When your gun goes "click" while the clock is running, you'll get quite adept at your malfunction routines!

International Defensive Pistol Association
www.idpa.com
Compete with "semi-realistic" self-defense scenarios. It's a great way to get in some fun practice with your carry or home-defense gun.

Single Action Shooting Society
www.sassnet.com
Yes, this is cowboy action shooting. Can you say pure fun? Lotsa old-style guns and competitors that call themselves names like Evil Roy, Black Bearded Bert and Molly Misfire.

Steel Challenge Shooting Association
www.steelchallenge.com
Lots of rounds downrange as fast as you can pull the trigger. You'll draw and shoot at steel plates and learn to love that satisfying "clang."

United States Practical Shooting Association
www.uspsa.org
The ultimate in run and gun. USPSA is all about lots of shooting, moving and speed. You'll see space-age race guns, but don't worry, there are classes where all competitors use stock equipment - like the gun you just bought!

Legal Stuff and Resources

In this country, the excuse of "not knowing the law" doesn't get you very far. So while we're including some links to resources to help you understand gun laws, you are always solely responsible for understanding local laws and regulations in your area. While "I don't recall" seems to be a perfectly acceptable defense strategy for elected officials, that plan doesn't work so well for us ordinary citizens.

Gun Laws Websites

USA Carry

www.usacarry.com

USA Carry was founded in 2007 as a resource to help concealed carriers understand state by state carry permits. It has since grown to a large community of over 50,000 forum users. The site includes concealed carry maps that show concealed carry permit reciprocity and state by state gun law summaries. USA Carry also includes directories of shooting instructors and gun ranges.

HandGunLaw.us

www.HandGunLaw.us

This site focuses on state by state gun laws and concealed carry permit reciprocity. If you want to know where your states' permit is valid, check here. Each state has a printable PDF document that summarizes gun laws. Better yet, the documents link directly to state statutes so you can see the raw legalese yourself.

NRA Institute for Legislative Action

www.nraila.org/gun-laws.aspx

It's worth spending some time exploring the NRA.org main site. From there you'll find the NRA-ILA web site which contains mountains of information on various state laws, recent legal challenges and relevant gun law articles from around the country.

CHAPTER 15 - Parting Shots

Be Safe and Have Fun!

We hope you enjoyed reading this book. It's intended to help relieve some of the apprehension and stress to finding, buying and shooting guns safely.

Most importantly, pay attention to the safety tips. Shooting is an incredibly safe pastime when people faithfully obey the four rules of gun safety.

Now go have fun!

About My Gun Culture

My Gun Culture is a half-cocked but right-on-target look at the world of shooting and all things related. If you want to learn, with a laugh, about guns, shooting products, personal defense, competition, industry news and the occasional Second Amendment issue, check us out at MyGunCulture.com.

Our literary assault team has developed contacts and access to the very depths of the shooting industry to bring you current and useful information with a side order of chuckle. From how-to's to interviews of industry figures to product reviews, we'll continue to bring you the latest and greatest from the industry.

Visit us at:

Mygunculture.com

www.facebook.com/mygunculture

www.twitter.com/mygunculture

www.pinterest.com/mygunculture

About the Author

Tom McHale was born helpless, hungry and shooting-deprived. He later discovered the joys of collecting and shooting guns, reloading ammunition and writing about his adventures with a healthy dose of fun.

Tom's career has been diverse, bordering on dysfunctional, with most of it spent leading marketing teams for a variety of technology companies including Microsoft and more than a couple of high-tech startups. He's finally seen the light and given up the corporate life to pursue his passion of creating educational, but slightly crazy, content related to guns, shooting, concealed carry and self defense. His most recent project is publishing a series of informative books under the Insanely Practical Guides brand. You can learn more at InsanelyPracticalGuides.com.

Also from Insanely Practical Guides...

Let's face it. Choosing the best way to carry a gun can be a daunting task. Whether you're new to guns or have been shooting since you were a wee tot, this book can help you understand concealed carry methods, how to carry a gun safely, and the relative pros and cons of over 120 specific holster models. We'll even teach you several ways to carry a gun in your underwear.

This book will help you make the right choice - saving you time and money - while offering a dose of humor while you learn.

Available at <u>Amazon.com</u>!

crossdressing
does not
infer
transgender
gay, or a
sexual
fetish

oct. 18
2013

coprophilia
albert
fish?
zoophilia